What
MENNONITES
Are
THINKING
–1998–

What
MENNONITES
Are
THINKING
–1998–

— Edited by —
Merle Good *and*
Phyllis Pellman Good

Good Books®
Intercourse, PA 17534

Design by Dawn J. Ranck

WHAT MENNONITES ARE THINKING, 1998

Copyright © 1998 by Good Books, Intercourse, PA 17534

International Standard Book Number: 1-56148-241-2
ISSN: 1099-0704

This book is made possible
in part by the following sponsors—

Eastern Mennonite University

The People's Place

Mennonite Weekly Review

Goshen College

Good Books

(Please read the sponsors' messages on pages 299 to 305.)

Acknowledgments

The book review by Marlin Adrian of **A Muslim and a Christian in Dialogue** is reprinted by permission of *Mennonite Life* (December, 1997) and Marlin Adrian.

"Race-related" by Anne Berry is reprinted by permission of Pinchpenny Press. Originally appeared in *Exposition 17* (1996).

"On This Earth" by Juanita Brunk is from the collection **Brief Landing on the Earth's Surface** and is reprinted by permission of The University of Wisconsin Press © 1996.

The book review by Susan Fisher Miller of **An Introduction to Old Order and Conservative Mennonite Groups** is reprinted by permission of Mennonite Weekly Review (July 24, 1997).

The "Conclusion" of **Women Against the Good War: Conscientious Objection and Gender on the American Home Front, 1941-1947** by Rachel Waltner Goossen is reprinted by permission of the publisher, University of North Carolina Press, © 1997.

"Ceremony" by Raylene Hinz-Penner is reprinted by permission of the author.

"Ana-Baptism" by Scott Holland is reprinted by permission of **Kairos: Arts and Letters of the Mennonite Culture.**

The book review by Gerlof D. Homan of *From Martyr to Muppy* is reprinted by permission of *Mennonite Quarterly Review* (April, 1996).

"The Water Table, There It Is" by Janet Kauffman is reprinted by permission of the author.

"'Center of Gravity' Now in the South" is reprinted by permission of Mennonite World Conference News Service.

The book review by Anne-Marie Klassen of **No Longer Alone: Mental Health and the Church** is reprinted by permission of the *Journal of Mennonite Studies* (Vol. 14, 1996).

"Excelsior" by Warren Kliewer is reprinted by permission of the author and *Mennonite Life* (December 1997).

The "Introduction" to **Scratching the Woodchuck; Nature on an Amish Farm** by David Kline is reprinted by permission of The University of Georgia Press © 1997.

Acknowledgments

"Passing" by Leonard N. Neufeldt is reprinted by permission of the author.

"For Trudy, My Aunt" and "In the Museum of the My Lai Massacre" by Barbara Nickel are from the collection **The Gladys Elegies** and are reprinted by permission of Coteau Books.

"Worshiping with the Early Anabaptists" by John Oyer and Keith Graber Miller is reprinted by permission of the authors and *Gospel Herald* (September, 1997).

"Rough-Cut Head" and "Gladiolus" by Keith Ratzlaff are from the collection **Man Under the Pear Tree** and are reprinted by permission of Anhinga Press.

The book review by John D. Roth of **Anabaptist History and Theology: An Introduction** is reprinted by permission of the Conrad Grebel Review (Fall, 1996).

The poem included in Marcus Shantz's Wedding Sermon is "Into the Midst" by Bronwen Wallace from the collection **Common Magic** and is reprinted by permission of Oberon Press © 1985.

The book review by Shirley H. Showalter of **A Community of Memory** is reprinted by permission of *Mennonite Quarterly Review* (October, 1996).

"Home on the Range in Lancaster, Where One Buffalo Still Roams" by Samuel S. Stoltzfus first appeared in *The Philadelphia Inquirer.* It is reprinted by permission of the author.

The book review by Gerald Studer of **Prayer Book for Earnest Christians** is reprinted by permission of *Pennsylvania Mennonite Heritage* (October, 1997).

"When Somalis Think of Canada, They Think 'Safe and Secure'" by Mohamud Siad Togane first appeared in *The Globe and Mail.* It is reprinted by permission of the author.

"Beyond the Blushes of Song of Songs" by Valerie S. Weaver is reprinted by permission of the author and *Gospel Herald* (October 14, 1997).

"When I Am Old, I Want to Be an Elder, Not a Senior" by Katie Funk Wiebe is reprinted by permission of the *MCC Women's Concerns Report* (September/October, 1997).

Table of Contents

Table of Contents

Introduction

We are pleased to present this collection for your consideration and enjoyment. Our goal has been to create an annual, containing some of the best current Mennonite writing and thinking.

"Mennonite" can mean faith, as accepted by certain groups of Christians who claim that name (Amish and Brethren are related groups). "Mennonite" can also bring to mind any of a variety of ways of life. This conversation/tension between faith and life forms the backdrop for many of the pieces in this collection.

Writings were selected on the basis of both content and style. For many pieces, this marks their first publication. All others, to qualify, were published since January 1, 1996.

Writers were eligible if they: a) are current members of a Mennonite-related group, or b) have had a significant interaction of many years with a Mennonite-related group, or c) deal with Mennonite-related material in a compelling way.

We hope readers of many backgrounds will enjoy this volume, including readers among our various Mennonite-related groups.

—*Merle Good and Phyllis Pellman Good, Editors*

Featured Articles, Essays, and Opinions, I

Race-related

by Anne Berry

"Have you ever been called a nigger?" my friend
Jodi asked me.

"No," I said. "What does that mean?"

"I'm not really sure, but there's a little black girl at
my school and people call her that sometimes."

I had been at Jodi's house after church, playing. I
was only seven or eight years old, and what she said
to me did not have much significance at the time. Yet,
I will never forget the conversation. I was puzzled as
to why she posed the question in the first place. How
was I associated with some other girl being called a
"nigger"? The word did not mean anything to me simply because I had never heard it used before.

The conversation I had at Jodi's house that day was
certainly not a traumatic experience. However, the
incident has put a definite time and place in my memory of my first run-in with the concept of racism. I do
not remember my parents ever sitting down with my
brother and sister and me to explain that we were "different." It was unnecessary. As I grew older, I learned
that "nigger" was a derogatory term and that bigotry
was "bad." The two words were part of something
called racism, and society was the culprit who forced
me to deal with it. I gradually caught on to the idea

that I was inevitably stuck somewhere in the middle of the whole mess.

Growing up in a family with a black father and a white mother never seemed out of the ordinary to me. I had a typical childhood and was raised in a typical home. I value the way my parents brought up Joe, Malinda, and me. They made sure all three of us were treated as fairly as possible and given the same opportunities as everyone else. We attended a private Mennonite high school as well as a private Mennonite college. We grew up in a safe and nurturing environment. We took swimming lessons and piano lessons just like our friends. I now find myself expecting to be treated like everyone else, whether or not I happen to be a few shades darker. By giving the general population the benefit of the doubt and assuming I will be treated equally, I have more confidence in my own ability to succeed in the world. It is not an issue of ignoring the racism which exists all around me, but refusing to let it dominate my outlook on life, and refusing to view all whites as individuals who are racist by nature.

Unfortunately for me, the problem is not as simple as I often like to make it appear. Classification of a person's race is frequently dependent upon her skin color, probably because it is the easiest way to categorize her. Referring to a person as "white," "black," or "Asian," does not leave room for exceptions. Juxtaposed, identity is not altogether cut-and-dried; it is not based solely on skin color. A person's behavior and mannerisms contribute to her identity as well. People who fall between specific groups are tossed around, attempting to find where they "fit in" socially and culturally.

I saw this issue of cultural identity reflected in society and the media before being aware that it applied to my own life. I was watching "Oprah" one day when she happened to have guests on her show who dated people of different races. Some black members of the audience praised and complimented the white guests who were attracted to black women or men. There was a young black woman, however, who said that she found white men more attractive because she had grown up in a predominantly white setting. This woman was verbally torn apart by some of the same black audience members, who treated her as if she was some sort of "traitor" to her own race. I was incensed. Granted, it had only been a talk show, but the attitudes of some of the people in the audience were frightening. Why was a white man who was consciously in pursuit of black women more acceptable than a black woman who happened to be attracted to white men due to the environment she was raised in? I was struck by the realization that racism is elusive because it manifests itself in a variety of forms, some more recognizable than others.

Black identity became a personal issue for me throughout my first year in college. Prior to this, I was comfortable being biracial. I was somewhere in the middle, but among my friends I had my "place," so to speak. Most of my friends and I had similar backgrounds, but they were always sensitive about the fact that, being a woman of color, I was unique. Since stepping onto a college campus, I feel as though I am on the defensive, trying to prove that I wholeheartedly accept myself as a "non-white" Mennonite living in a predominantly white culture.

I have often struggled with the question, "What does it mean to be black?" I tend to believe that blackness comes from African ancestry, having roots within the traditional black culture, and simply being born into a black family. My father, his mother and father, and their mothers and fathers are what make me black. This being the case, is there anything that could ever make me less than black? If I were to answer "No" to my own question, I would be ignoring an unspoken truth; in our society, a person must now meet certain social or even economic criteria to be considered truly black. The idea still exists that in order for a person to be truly black, she must be engulfed in an impoverished, crime-ridden, and stereotypical "black culture."

I do not have any regrets about being who I am or living in the kind of environment I do. I only regret that other people cannot understand that I am satisfied with my ethnicity and my part in society. At times, it is difficult to stand on middle ground. I frequently remind myself that I do not have to lump myself with one race group or another, merely because others choose to do so. No amount of poking or prodding nor influence from black or white society is enough to completely upset my fruit basket.

I find it ridiculous, therefore, that at college there is more pressure for me to identify with one side or the other. In effect, I am being asked to choose whether I am black or white. The pressure is subtle, but it exists nonetheless. I am generally considered black because of my skin color. I have grown up in a white Mennonite culture, and the majority of my friends are white. Because of this, I often feel that other black students view me as another product of the white man's culture, a black woman who lacks knowledge or understanding of her true black heritage. By acting "white" and talking "white," I am somehow less of a black person. I have always taken pride in my multi-ethnic background. For this reason, I am saddened by the fact that other people expect me to behave a certain way because of my outward appearance. I find it ironic that when I am with my cousins—be it my black cousins or my white cousins—I am just one of the family; another Berry, another Hostetler. My race is obviously part of me, but I am not convinced that the white side or the black side defines my whole being. Both sides of the family make up a part of my culture. It may not be obvious in the way I talk or the way I walk; it is, however, most undoubtedly existent in the very core of my being.

I am proud, as a white Mennonite, to have such a fascinating history. I am proud, as an African American, to have such an inspiring heritage. These are two distinct characteristics that have created me. They have shaped me to become a mix and swirl of combinations of ideas, thoughts, and experiences that transcend color lines.

My friend and I used to walk into stores and I would pretend to start crying while she would say, "Just because you're adopted, you think you can have anything you want!" For the two of us, it was the funniest thing in the world: to play off the preconceived ideas of others. I must admit that I take delight in defying society's stereotypes. I also enjoy shopping with my mother—a brown young woman next to an older white woman—wondering if the other shoppers are thrown for a loop when I call out to her: "Hey, Mom, can I get this sweater?"

Anne Berry is a student at Goshen (Indiana) College.

Tea Parties and Peacemakers
by James C. Juhnke

December 16, 1997, is the two hundred and twenty-fourth anniversary of the Boston Tea Party. This year I have decided not to celebrate.

Not that I ever have made myself up as a Mohawk on December 16 and whooped up a storm in memory of Samuel Adams and his brave tea-dumpers.

But this year is different. This time my non-celebration is intentional. Instead, I will light a candle in memory of an event I only recently discovered: the great Philadelphia Tea Non-Party.

In late 1773 while Boston was whipping up its froth of violence that led to King George III's crackdown on the colonies, Philadelphia found a way to resolve its Tea Crisis nonviolently. When the tea-bearing ship *Polly* reached Delaware Bay, the Philadelphians refused its cargo as surely as had the Bostonians. But they resisted nonviolently. The Quaker merchants persuaded the British captain, Samuel Ayres, to take the tea back to London. They smoothed the way by advancing funds to buy supplies for the journey. John Penn, the proprietary governor, treated the situation with benign neglect, unlike Thomas Hutchinson in Boston who forced a showdown with the anti-British hotheads.

Huzzah for the Philadelphia Tea Non-Party! If we want to know how to resolve conflicts peaceably, we should look to Philadelphia. If we want to know how to start a war, we should attend the Boston Tea Party. I have read that some people are prepared to spend millions of dollars to dredge up a few decayed fragments of these tea boxes from the Boston harbor and treat them as holy relics. What would it take to rescue the successes of conflict resolution in our history from the muck and mire of collective amnesia?

American history as we know it prepares our imaginations for war, not for peace. We learn in school that the War for Independence was not only exciting but inevitable. We don't learn about the peace heroes—those who persistently worked for peace. We have not heard, for example, about Joseph Galloway.

Galloway was a Pennsylvania leader who came to the First Continental Congress in 1774 with a plan to reform the British empire and end taxation without representation. He proposed to create an American branch of Parliament, a "Grand Council" with members to be appointed by the colonial assemblies. The "Grand Council" would have had veto power over all British legislation for the colonies. Galloway's plan had much support at the Congress. It failed to pass by one vote. Some opponents could not imagine that provinces as diverse as Massachusetts and Virginia could cooperate under an American parliament. They mistakenly thought King George would back down if they refused to compromise.

We cannot know the outcomes of paths not taken. Perhaps Galloway's plan, if adopted, would only have delayed the approach of war. But the vote on the plan is a historical fact. If our challenge today is to avoid war rather than make new ones, it is the sort of fact that deserves our attention. Wars are not always inevitable. Nothing refutes the inevitability of war as convincingly as the cases of wars that did not happen. At every stage of American history, persistent peacemakers worked to manage conflict and avoid war—often with success we ignore. In 1799-1800 President John Adams courageously backed away from an impending war with France, even though he knew well that the outbreak of peace would hurt the political future of his Federalist party. In 1807 President Thomas Jefferson had good cause to go to war against England, but chose a nonviolent strategy of economic embargo instead. The embargo did avoid war, but our history textbooks invariably treat it as a failure.

Adams and Jefferson, like other leaders of the new republic, assumed that war-making belonged to monarchies and their corrupt conspiracies with militaristic aristocracies. A "standing army" was a threat to peace. Adams called it a "many-bellied monster" which devoured the national treasury. These men knew that republicanism and militarism did not mix. Nearly two centuries later, President Eisenhower warned against the power of the military industrial complex in American life. Ike's warning stood in a noble American tradition.

The American peace tradition remains on the dimmest margins of our historical consciousness. In public school, on national holidays, and on the TV history channel, we learn that the United States is a country made by war. We all know the names of great war heroes—Washington, Grant, Lee, Tecumseh, Crazy

Horse—but our peace heroes are forgotten. At our mall bookstores, books on military history merit separate sections which have more selections than all other topics in American history combined. How can we learn the truth that the builders and peacemakers in our history have outnumbered the destroyers and warriors?

The American constituency for peace and conflict resolution is small, but it is growing. In recent years public schools all across our land have begun peer mediation programs. They recruit and train students to mediate conflicts on the playground and in classrooms. The peace principles they learn are basic: Take time to cool off; listen to your opponent's viewpoint; think of possible alternatives. These principles have helped resolve conflicts peaceably throughout American history.

My candle for the Philadelphia Tea Non-Party of 1773 will be a flicker of hope. I pray that the post-Cold War generation may learn that America has a history of peace as well as war. May they find their greater inspiration in the memory of Joseph Galloway, Deganawidah, Elihu Burrit, Jeanette Rankin, Martin Luther King, Jr., and the great cloud of peace witnesses who have enriched our common history.

James C. Juhnke teaches history at Bethel (North Newton, Kansas) College and has written several books and dramas.

Scratching the Woodchuck: Nature on an Amish Farm

by David Kline

I grew up on the farm where I now live with my wife and children. The farm rests at the edge where the gently rolling hills of the Allegheny plateau begin to flatten out into the table land of northwestern Ohio; where the eastern hardwoods begin to give way to the cottonwoods and burr oaks and prairie lands; where joe-pye weed meets black-eyed Susan. From here to the southeast, hill country extends to the Atlantic coastal plain and, beginning 20 miles to the northwest, flat land reaches all the way to the foothills of the Rockies.

Of course, when I was growing up there were no coastal plains or Rockies, at least not until fifth-grade geography. My world consisted of farmlands in a radius of about four miles from home—a distance that could be walked or biked in several hours.

In that circle were perhaps 50 farms with a variety of livestock and a patchwork of fields, two villages, and several country schools. One of these, Elm Grove, a one-room public school, so named but shaded by a massive white oak, was eight-tenths of a mile south and half a mile west of our farm. A walk that could take anywhere from 15 minutes to two hours, depending on the weather and the season. It was here at Elm Grove, surrounded by rich fields and woodlands and within a quarter mile of an interesting bog, that I spent eight glorious school years and where my love for nature was nurtured.

My teacher for seven of those years, for grades two through eight, was Clarence F. Zuercher, the finest naturalist I have ever met. Interestingly, Mr. Zuercher had also been my father's teacher for the second through the eighth grades, 40 years before in another part of the county. My interest in nature was planted before I entered school, but under Mr. Zuercher's tutelage it sprouted and grew.

Mr Zuercher, the son of Swiss immigrants, had a broad knowledge of the natural world, and he immersed us in the flora and fauna of the local watershed from September through May. From birds and reptiles to trees and wildflowers to butterflies and moths, nothing escaped his sharp eyes. We learned to identify all the species of local trees not only by the shape of their leaves but also by the look and texture of their bark and by their fruits. Mr. Zuercher also had a keen interest in the fishes of the local waterways.

A creek, the Salt, ran from southeast to northwest about a mile north of the schoolhouse. It meandered for half a mile across the western end of our pasture field. The creek was spring fed, clear, and fast flowing, dropping 10 feet per mile, but it harbored many deep and mysterious pools that made superb fishing and swimming holes.

Oftentimes in early April our teacher would dismiss school half an hour early. In his '52 Ford he headed for the creek to fish for black suckers. And he was an expert at it. He elevated sucker fishing to an art.

One spring he took three of us boys along to try our

luck at sucker fishing. Since the schoolhouse was at the outer edge of the Killbuck watershed, Mr. Zuercher traveled several miles downstream where the creek was wider and deeper and even more alluring than it was on our farm. Even the snakes were bigger. Our communication was by gesture and whisper. He scoffed at expensive tackle and fished with a cane pole. While we tried our best, and caught a few, he kept hauling them in. We were in the presence of a master fisherman who understood fish as well as he did the shenanigans of schoolboys.

While we were fishing he pointed out a soaring red-tailed hawk overhead and nesting kingfishers in a streambank burrow nearby. Also, a yellow warbler in an old willow. Soon choretime came, and we had to leave because Mr. Zuercher, besides being a teacher and fisherman and naturalist, was also a farmer. The cows had to be milked.

When I was 10 years old, spring on the farm did not begin with the fieldwork; it began with sucker fishing in that wonderful creek. That could be anywhere from late March through mid-April when the black suckers began actively feeding.

To us, sucker fishing was stealth fishing, unlike the carefree bobber fishing for rock bass and bluegill later in the spring and in the clockless summer. One had to tread softly on the creek bank lest the wary fish would detect your footfall, hide in the tangles of underwater tree roots, and refuse to take your bait, no matter how enticingly the earthworm wiggled in front of their downturned mouths.

It took skill to catch suckers in the clear and cold waters of early spring, when the single track of the freshwater mussel showed as plainly on the unmarked sand of the creek bottom as a white chalk mark on a clean blackboard. If the fish weren't spooked, they would start at the head of the earthworm and slowly suck it up. When the line began moving toward the deep dark mysterious root-tangled part of the hole, where the sunning water snakes had dropped into only minutes before, and goose bumps of anticipation crept up your arm, you set the hook and hauled the resisting fish to the bank. The suckers had tough sinewy mouths, and once they were hooked they stayed hooked. Bass would sometimes shake loose the hook, and we made diving leaps to grab a flopping fish before it regained the safety of the water, where it surely wouldn't take a bait again. On good days several dozen suckers could be caught.

As the water warmed, the suckers seemed to disappear, and our attention turned to rock bass and bluegill and horned chubs. These were less wary fish, and fishing for them was more carefree. We could slosh bare feet in the water, and the fish kept on biting. The season of summer officially arrived, not on the summer solstice, but when the water became warm enough for swimming. That occurred sometime in early June, when the water snakes began shying away from the heat of midday and sought shade instead. Along with the heat of the season came hay making and small-grain harvest—threshing time—which meant more work for us and less time for woods and creek snooping.

At the end of three months of summer vacation and after harvest, we could hardly wait for school to begin in early September. Most of us were at the schoolhouse on opening morning long before Mr. Zuercher arrived a little before 8:30 and unlocked the door. We scrambled over the newly oiled wood floor to find choice desks near windows or the back door or next to the tanned skin of the red fox; we unpacked our pencils and other school necessities and fled for the ball diamond for 10 minutes of play before the bell rang. Regardless of where we settled, Mr. Zuercher moved each of us a desk forward every month.

But he never let the classroom interfere with our education. I can't recall my class ever getting through a textbook before the school year ended in late May. At that time every eighth grade student had to pass a state exam in order to graduate. When my class was in the eighth grade and preparing for that dreaded test of 200 questions, Mr. Zuercher told us that he didn't have much time to devote to us, but that we should read, read, and read. He would send us out to his car so that we could study uninterrupted by the other classes, and one dog, sharing the single room. Of course, he sent the keys along so that we could listen to the radio. Usually, Elizabeth, the only girl in our class, would have the front seat, and so naturally we boys endured the country music she preferred. We thought it was silly that every mournful singer either lost his dog or his car or his girlfriend.

Mr. Zuercher believed that all of nature was part of the web of life. From the delicate maidenhair fern and reptiles to the birds of prey and hordes of insects that shared our farms. He insisted that each filled an important niche in the rich diversity of life and he taught us to tread lightly on the land. "Give more back than you take," he said. "And don't pay too much attention to the agricultural experts," he cautioned us. Since all of his

45 or so students in the eight grades were from farms, we took his advice seriously.

From Mr. Zuercher I learned to see the natural world as a boundless adventure. There was no end to the discoveries and beauty to be found beneath rocks, in the creek, in the woods, in the sky, and in humans. (When a student gazing out one of the windows spotted a Goodyear blimp, classes were dismissed, and everybody went outside to watch the huge airship crawl through the sky as slowly as a snail crossing the road. The day-dreaming student was praised for his keen sense of observation.)

One of the reasons I immersed myself in nature was that throughout my eight years in that one-room school, I stuttered. Severely enough that I had a constant gut-gnawing fear of speaking in front of my class. In the woods I had no such fears—the trees and flowers and birds and moths and butterflies and frogs and snakes and clouds and stars never laughed at me. To me, the God that created all that beauty and grace must be a wonderful and loving Being. Nature became a sanctuary, a solace, for me. A realm of limitless love.

Perhaps my fear of speech during my adolescent years turned me to writing. I became fascinated by words that I could write or read but could never utter in front of people. To the trees and wild creatures, yes, but never to humans. Those 26 letters of the alphabet above the blackboard intrigued me. So did the dictionary. There were infinite ways, I thought, to arrange words to describe the boundless beauty and mystery beyond the doorstep.

Sometime during those formative years in grade school I began keeping a daily diary. The daily entries were short, often a terse "Went to school"; "Played ball and walked to the woods"; "Saw a sparrow hawk kill a cardinal"; "Had our Christmas program. Levi was Scrooge. My gift: a pocketknife and a flashlight."

It wasn't until I was drafted in the mid-sixties, in my late teens, and worked in a Cleveland hospital, that I began serious journal writing. Page after page of human activities. There seemed to be a dearth of nature in the city, at least when compared with the country. But then I had access to a telephone, and so I called the Audubon Rare Bird Alert almost daily to find out whether there were any jaegers or rare gulls hanging out along the lakeshore. Or perhaps a snowy owl at Burke Lakefront Airport, or a Townsend's solitaire at a city birdfeeder. These rare birds and some common chickadees and the spring's first dandelions, and of course, the city's fine snowstorms, found their way into my journal.

When I moved to the city I looked forward to the change of scenery, the throb of humanity, easy access to a well-stocked library, and by not having those morning and evening barn chores, time to read. But I wasn't prepared for the cultural shock that followed. While the sounds in the country tend to be soft, muted, and musical, city sounds were harsh: tires squealing, shouts in the night, and a constant wailing of sirens. Someone injured, dying, a fire, a stabbing—which meant work for me in the hospital. I could help those unfortunate victims of the city.

Another part of the city life I found bewildering at first was how people constantly complained about the weather. It was either too hot or too cold or too wet. Even if it was extremely dry and the crops and gardens desperately needed moisture, the weatherman would say that the weekend would be miserable because of the threat of rain. For me, coming from a culture that was so closely tied to the land and the weather and the rhythms of the seasons, their attitudes were absurd.

At home no one complained about the weather. After all, God controlled everything, the sun, the clouds, the wind, and the rain. Complaining was finding fault with God, we were told. My dad would tell the tragic story of his Swiss immigrant neighbor who cursed the weather. One early summer day while Charlie was cultivating corn a thunderstorm came up. He sought shelter in the chicken house. Maybe he shook his fist at the sky as he sometimes did. In any event, lightning struck the building and Charlie died.

In time I settled into city life. I found my way to the public library, visited the museums, attended different churches, and went downtown to sit on park benches and watch people. They were always in a hurry, head down, briefcase in hand, rushing everywhere. Never had I felt more alone, sitting on those cold steel park benches, even though I was surrounded by people.

Part of the difference between city and country was that in the country we tend to see God in every aspect of creation. Likely because most of the things in our lives are God-created: the grass, the trees, the birds and mammals, and the people. In the city so much is human-created: concrete, asphalt, glass, steel on rubber, industrial smoke, and those ugly tangles of overhead electrical wires. Why, I thought, if you could live in the country, would anyone choose to live in the city?

I found out that in the city, even more than in the country where many houses are never locked, the home became a sanctuary. A place, once the dead bolts were secured, where one went to escape that "out there"; where family and friends assembled within the security of one another. It was in the homes where I learned that urban people are very much like rural people—they care, laugh, and worship the same God. Maybe not the omnipresent God of my rural community, but the same one nevertheless. And I found out that there are angels in the city.

I moved to Cleveland in late November, and when I was returning after spending the Christmas holiday at home, the Greyhound bus got caught in one of the early winter snowstorms northeastern Ohio is famous for. Arriving three hours late, in the early morning hours, the city was at a standstill. The city buses, my usual mode of travel to my apartment eight miles out in a suburb (for 35 cents), had quit for the night, and there were no taxis running. The city was asleep.

Since I did not have enough money for a hotel room and sleeping in the bus station wasn't an option, I walked into the howling fury of the storm. Almost immediately car lights came out of the swirling snow and stopped by the curb; the driver reached over and opened the passenger door.

"Do you need help, or a ride?" a voice asked.

"Indeed I do, but I have almost no money," I said.

After the driver said it was no problem, I got in the car, and we headed, alone on the wide streets, for my new home. The driver, an African American with some gray in his hair, said he had woken at 1:00 a.m. and hearing the storm outside could not go back to sleep. He thought someone might be needing help, so he got in his car and drove to the bus station.

Finally, after numerous U-turns on the slippery roads, we reached the street where I lived. He did not want to take any money for the ride, but I insisted and gave him all I had. As I watched the tail lights of his car fade into the storm, my eyes welled with tears of gratitude for this angel of mercy.

That man forever changed my view of the city. I realized that love can live in the human heart anywhere. I knew that the Good Samaritan was alive and well.

When my work in the city was finished, I came back to my boyhood home, to the farm, and discovered that the quietude bothered me. But it did not take long to recover and rediscover the beauty and the pleasures of nature on the farm.

When I walked to the barn in the early morning, bright and lovely Venus was there in the eastern sky to greet me, instead of being lost in the haze of a city's light pollution. And when I plowed again in early spring, I watched a kestrel "rung upon the rein of a wimpling wing" hover above a meadow vole, and then swiftly drop, talons flared, for a meal. I was reunited to the natural world and returned to the natural rhythms of the seasons—the memory of the land came rushing back.

I could look at the farm and its inhabitants through the eyes of a stranger and began to see things I had missed before. Didn't Emerson write that a man standing in his own field is unable to see it? Before my return I had never seen the courtship flight of the horned lark, so common yet so elusive, in our fields. This past spring, as I have in many springs past, I watched the male lark perform his rite of spring. I was planting corn when he took flight from the tilled field.

Singing and circling until he was 500 feet above the team and me, the lark serenaded his mate, and us, for 15 minutes before dropping back to earth.

On my homecoming to the farm, every tree, every bird, every flower, every insect, was just as vivid and interesting and mysterious as it was during those days at the one-room school. Of course, by that time, every one-room public school in Ohio was forced by the State Board of Education to close its doors. The antiquated system wasn't providing an adequate education for its students, the board proclaimed. Our school district had seven schools, which had their last classes and nature walks in 1960; they were then consolidated into one school. For the first time the school district had to buy buses, and within a few years our small district was gobbled up by a larger district: that typical scenario of a small fish being swallowed by a bigger one and so on down the line. But as Bill McKibben said, "Bigger means only bigger, it doesn't mean better."

As far as literature goes, my passion for nature was probably more stirred by those pocket-sized Golden Nature Guides that our teacher kept on hand than any other book. He had four—trees, wildflowers, butterflies and moths, and birds. In the late 1950s our county bought a bookmobile, "The Traveling Bookshelf," which made its rounds to the rural schools every six weeks. Then, my natural history reading expanded dramatically and included Jack London, Thornton Burgess, and Edwin Way Teale. It wasn't, however, until I returned from the city that I "discovered" the writings of Aldo Leopold, Hal Borland, John Hay, Wendell Berry, and countless other great writers.

I continued to write in my journals about nature on

the farm and eventually sort of fell into writing for publication. A friend loaned me a book, *Communicating the Outdoor Experience.* Even though the book was intended for rod and gun writers, it taught me a great deal on how to write for publication.

The last time I visited Mr. Zuercher, he was in his eighties and housebound for the first time in his life. He told me in a voice reduced to a whisper by the ravages of Parkinson's disease, "Nature is so interesting. You are never too old to enjoy it. I never went on a walk that I didn't see or find something exciting and interesting. In Proverbs we read that 'It is the glory of God to conceal things, but it is our glory to search things out.' Over the years I have searched out many things." Then he smiled.

David Kline is a farmer and writer from Fredericksburg, Ohio.

"Center of Gravity"
Now in the South

by Marshall V. King

For the first time in the history of the Anabaptist-Mennonite movement, its baptized followers number more than one million.

The Mennonite and Brethren in Christ World Directory 1998, published by Mennonite World Conference (MWC), shows 1.06 million baptized members, according to Larry Miller, MWC executive secretary. The members are in 192 conferences in 60 countries.

The 1994 census showed 973,921 members in 194 bodies in 61 countries. The increase is about 85,000 members, or 8.7 percent.

The worldwide church directory four years ago showed, for the first time, more Anabaptist-related Christians in the southern part of the globe than in the north. That trend is continuing, Miller said. The significant thing is that the center of gravity is in the south, he said.

Africa, Asia, and Central and South America are home to 582,000 members. The number of members in North America and Europe is 477,000.

Younger churches are growing faster than those whose origins are nearer the birth of Anabaptism. The first of the younger churches were established in Indonesia and India in the 19th century, Miller said. Most of the churches growing quickly were established in the 20th century.

This is happening to other denominations as well, Miller commented. The numerical center of Christianity as a whole is shifting.

Most churches in Europe are not growing. The increase of 12,754 members in Europe is due to the larger number of *Umsiedler*—immigrants from the former Soviet Union—counted this time in independent congregations in Germany. Without this statistical adjustment, the European number would have been smaller than in 1994.

North America appears to be following the trend of slower growth, but many don't recognize the shift. North Americans in particular don't think about it, Miller remarked. He predicts that before the middle of the next century, churches in the south will play the primary role in shaping the direction of the Anabaptist-Mennonite movement.

Still, the six countries with the largest membership have not changed in the past four years (see chart on page 29).

Zimbabwe joined the list of countries with more than 20,000 members, which also includes Germany, Mexico, Paraguay, and Tanzania.

Mozambique, with 22,900 members in 1994, is not included in this year's *World Directory* since the church there is no longer associated with the Brethren in Christ.

Many of the figures reported by national conferences are only estimates. Attempts are made to verify accuracy if questions arise. This year's census takes into account the fact that some congregations hold multiple conference memberships, particularly North American congregations.

Membership increased on each continent by these percentages: Africa, 16.66; Asia and the Pacific, 3.98; Central and South America, 12.09; Europe, 25.95; North America, 2.02.

Marshall V. King is a staff writer for Mennonite World Conference, living in Elkhart, Indiana.

Anabaptist-Mennonite World Membership

Top 10 Countries	1998	1994
United States	287,345	287,781
Congo	175,837	136,200
Canada	128,633	117,932
India	87,466	84,195
Indonesia	62,823	60,709
Ethiopia	57,011	50,018
Germany	39,610	24,414
Tanzania	32,100	19,486
Paraguay	25,009	22,512
Mexico	20,689	20,478
Continents		
North America	415,978	405,713
Africa	322,708	276,653
Asia/Pacific	157,075	151,057
Latin America	102,496	91,436
Europe	61,886	49,132
Total	1,060,000	973,921
Countries	60	61
Conferences	192	194

An Apple Tree, or Mango
by Shirley Kurtz

Back when my husband was taking his physics, botany, biochemistry, microbiology, mammalogy, genetics, and physiology courses at Penn State, I managed to remain clueless about science. I could maybe spell some of the terminology and knew what mammals were and perhaps amphibians and reptiles, and geology had to do with rocks, but I never thought in terms of *phyllum, organism, species*. I was aware at one point that he was trapping shrews of all things and storing them in our freezer for a class requirement. Perhaps it seems odd that a wife could be so ignorant about her husband's studies; on the other hand, the husband buried in his work wasn't thinking about *Hamlet* and *Macbeth, Spoon River Anthology, Our Town*—the kind of material I loved and was teaching to high schoolers (for some reason I avoided grammar and composition). So in a way it was tit-for-tat.

Then after Paulson began teaching junior-highers at a Mennonite school near Mount Joy, not only dispensing all his facts about atoms and molecules and protozoans and DNA but also brewing chemicals atop Bunsen burners and taking the students to a nearby farm pond to scoop out slimy creatures, or the farm breeders' cooperative in Lancaster to see the bulls used for artificial insemination (another place they went, calf embryos were being surgically implanted in cows—it wasn't just the birds and the bees they were talking about in school), I had only half an ear tuned. Oh, his stories were funny. Crawling through Mummau's cave with students he'd nearly gotten stuck in a tight passageway and panicked, he told me afterwards, but I was more worried about how to get the mud off his pants.

Busy with our children at home and predisposed to more literary matters, words in and of themselves, I had them feasting on the lore of the ages (well, maybe this is stretching it): *Harry and the Terrible Whatzit, Mike Mulligan's Steam Shovel, Blueberries for Sal, The Biggest Bear, Paddle-to-the-Sea, In the Night Kitchen*— whatever treasures I could find at the public library and cart home. Although a good story didn't have to be outright true, I wasn't overly fond of Mother Goose; maybe the rhymes were to nonsensical. And I crafted my own tales when I could, in snatched moments. The stuff in Paulson's books, though, anything science related, held no interest for me. Any of his commentary on mutation, photosynthesis, symbiosis, homeostasis, or whatever went in one ear and out the other. Disinclined toward nature, by nature, I wasn't paying attention; I wasn't really listening.

As Paulson later explained, he usually skipped the chapter on evolution in the seventh grade textbook because there wasn't time for everything, but occasionally in the morning devotions with those students he held forth on the subject.

Of course, I wasn't sitting in on this.

"We have the accounts in Genesis," said the teacher; propped against the blackboard, he slowly twirled his chalk. "Michael, please don't lean back like that in your chair. You all know the stories. 'And God said, "Let there be light," and there was light.' Then firmament, and dry land and seas, vegetation, the heavenly bodies, fish and birds, creeping crawling things and legged beasts, people—'and it was very good.'

"Those creation stories," the teacher continued, pacing now and restless, "were a kind of poetry passing down from generation to generation; they satisfied the curiosity of primitive peoples. Today, though, scientists aren't content with a few verses in Genesis." His arms commenced to flap, and Stacey and Marcella in the front seats closest to his desk exchanged wary looks. "They study all the little bits of natural evidence and develop theories based on the evidence. Scientists are saying now that long ago there was a Big Bang, and afterwards chaos, and then the clumping of planet and stars.

"But it was just hazy light, in the beginning," the teacher explained. "Please, Michael—your chair. The sunshine was diffused by all the swirling matter coming together in clumps. Gradually land separated from atmosphere on our planet and life emerged—first sea life and then land forms of life.

"And this is what I find so intriguing." Here the teacher came to an abrupt halt, but his arms were flapping wildly. "If you compare evolutionary theory and the biblical stories, you'll notice some interesting parallels. The fossil records in the scriptures indicate a similar sequence in development. Light, and then sun, moon, and stars. Water creatures first, and then land creatures. It's almost as if modern science is corroborating those ancient accounts!"

The teacher's chalk suddenly escaped his clutch and sailed across the room. "We really don't know how God created the universe, but maybe we're cracking the riddle."

No, I wasn't there myself, hanging onto his every word.

I don't know exactly when—early in his eleventh year at the Mennonite school—Paulson first mentioned his plans for a presentation at an upcoming PTA. But I was suddenly attentive. "Oh, no!" I exclaimed. "You'll get yourself in trouble."

"Nah," Paulson argued. "I'm not worried. I've already checked with the principal. It'll be okay. I'll be speaking to just the parents of the seventh graders, in my classroom." Two or three mothers in the past few years had approached him with concerns—their children had come home talking about evolution—and he'd sat down and explained things and they'd seemed mollified, so he was thinking he could prevent further trouble with this presentation. He honestly believed if he distributed his charts and pointed out various analogies and people *understood* . . .

So of course afterwards I blamed him.

What an uproar, with upset patrons telephoning school board members now to complain *(the teaching of evolution in a Christian school, buzz, buzz)* and the school board scheduling special sessions and grilling Paulson.

"This is The Inquisition," I hissed privately. "We won't quibble about a literal six-day creation," board members said. "And animals and plants evolving—that's no big deal. But man was definitely created special, in the image of God." "Why, yes," agreed Paulson. "But we don't know all the details. The Bible isn't a science text." How I smarted at the gossip and suspicions and accusations—and he'd started all this! He'd brought up the subject!

From somewhere or other, maybe an anthology up on our bookshelf, I found a poem for the children to learn:

If Wisdom's ways you wisely seek,

Five things observe with care:

Of whom you speak,

To whom you speak,

And how, and when, and where.

Perhaps my literary instincts were running amok, for I also put the children to memorizing scriptures: "Happy are you when people hate you, reject you . . ." Paulson maintained that people had every right to act according to their convictions and to protect their children from error, and indeed he had a point, but long after he was formally dismissed from his job and we moved to West Virginia I raged.

One thing, though, I didn't much care to admit. Like all those good folks we'd left behind in Pennsylvania, I'd grown up on those Genesis accounts—*garden, snake, fig leaves*, the images were deeply embedded in my soul—and while it hardly seemed likely, anymore, that God actually knelt along a river and patted out a mud man and then gave him mouth-to-mouth resuscitation or whatever to start him breathing, the other possibility—our having descended from outright animals or those hunched, loping, slanty-headed monsters in books—was deeply unsettling. "Day" meaning "age" in the beginning verses—this made sense enough. But those hideous Cro-Magnons!

However, I couldn't believe I'd married a heretic.

Well, it was much too complex and involved to worry about. I'd have to focus on other things. I'd just think up some more stories.

Her husband taught in a public school now, but the woman still barely glanced at the piles of notebooks and tests he hauled home to grade. Any mention of protoplasm, black holes, ecosystems, energy, matter, and so on, she heard only dimly, preoccupied as she was with her reading and story writing and agonizing revisions. One evening at the supper table he told about an experiment in class: A kid named Jason—he'd changed first into old clothes—had jumped into a 50-gallon drum half full of water; the point was to measure his volume. Other students had drawn the high-water mark with him submerged, and then after Jason had climbed out they'd poured in jugful after jugful of water, keeping track of how many jugs it took to bring the water level up to the mark. Jason's volume had been 40 gallons, or else it was 80. Well, she could see how her husband was a good teacher. But the woman herself remained woefully ignorant despite his best efforts; the time he tried valiantly to explain the difference between weight and mass she went all limp inside and hopeless—it was just too complicated.

Clearly, she'd always been unscientific beyond description.

"Todd!" she'd screech on school mornings (only the youngest child was still at home, and even he understood about mass and other weighty scientific terms), "You'll be late for your bus!" Soon the house was entirely silent; she could mull and stew in peace. Seven-thirty a.m. was too early for her to be actually attacking a manuscript—she was still too foggy—so first she'd finish her Bible reading, plus maybe that piece in *Newsweek* she'd gotten only halfway through last night. And then if she did a little dusting next, something active to get her blood running and her brain in gear, she could soon be plotting and weaving and contriving all the juicy little details.

One morning in late winter, with the fog dissipating some, already, because she'd gotten her dusting out of the way first for a change, she pored over the beginning chapters in Genesis. Perhaps the steady coursing of red sea through vein was firing the imagination, for she could almost hear the ancient storyteller's chanting:

And there was evening, and there was morning—the first day . . . And there was evening, and there was morning—the second day . . . And there was evening, and there was morning—the third day . . . And God saw that it was good.

The tribal elder reciting would have been bony and gnarled, she decided, and as he rocked on his haunches his voice rose and fell in singsong tones:

> When the Lord God made the earth
> and the heavens—and no shrub of the
> field had yet appeard on the earth and
> no plant of the field had yet sprung up—
> the Lord God formed the man from the
> dust of the ground and breathed into his
> nostrils the breath of life.

"Gabuudhie gabuudhie, ayeeeeeee," the listeners
circling close chorused in agreement (for some
reason the whole scene popped up African in her
head instead of Mesopotamian, with everybody's
necks encased tightly in beads and their bellies
circled by clanking coins strung on lengths of
frayed rope).

Each line in its turn served as metaphor for
truth beyond comprehension; the storyteller coming to this next part lowered his voice and his
audience hushed:

> Now the Lord God had planted a gar-
> den in the east, in Eden; and there he
> put the man he had formed. And the
> Lord God made all kinds of trees grow
> out of the ground—trees that were pleas-
> ing to the eye and good for food. In the
> middle of the garden were the tree of life
> and the tree of the knowledge of good
> and evil.

Funny, how as a child she'd pictured these as real
trees bearing, oh, say, apples or pears; she hadn't
known about kiwi, papayas, mangoes. She'd
thought Eve had handed Adam a literal piece of
fruit with seeds in it, off a tree called knowledge—

Oh, my word!

In the absolute silence of her house, the woman nearly gasped.

She didn't bring up the matter till after supper, though. Todd had wolfed his dessert and left the kitchen, but her husband was only now unhooking his feet from the rungs of his chair. She turned toward him eagerly. "That one tree in the Garden of Eden, you know? The knowledge of good and evil? Was this maybe the acquiring of intellect? Cro-Magnon or—"

"Crow who? Oh. Cro-Magnon."

Her husband blinked several times and studied her gravely.

"That never ever occured to me," he said finally.

"'How Cro-Magnon Got His Brain.' You know, like 'How the Elephant Got His Trunk.' You read that one to Todd—you said you wanted to do the reading for a change. 'In the High and Far-Off times the Elephant, O Best Beloved, had no trunk. He had only a blackish, bulgy nose, as big as a boot, that he could wriggle about from side to side; but he couldn't pick up things with it . . .'"

"'Led go! You are hurtig be!'" her husband mused, remembering. "Todd begged me to read it again. And then he wondered how far up noseholes go."

Her husband was going on now about sphenoidal sinuses and spheno-ethnoidal recesses and nasopalatine nerves, textbook stuff he still retained from that physiology course at Penn State, but the woman only smiled. As she pushed back her chair and collected a few dirty plates to carry to the sink, she was already tuning out. She couldn't wait to get back to that story she'd worked on all day, soon as the fog lifted tomorrow morning.

Shirley Kurtz is a writer who lives in Keyser, West Virginia.

Women Against the Good War: A Summary

by Rachel Waltner Goossen

During the 1940s American mobilization for war was a conservative operation in virtually every aspect, including the persistence of sex segregation both in the military sector and on the home front. Civilian Public Service, created by the federal government and administered by historic peace churches, reflected the conventional gender ideology of the era. Federally sanctioned provisions for conscientious objectors were directed solely toward men. As the alternative service program evolved, CPS administrators assumed that women would contribute in their habitual role as providers of moral and emotional support. In short, the architects of alternative service never envisioned that so many women would ultimately contribute to the program in so many ways.

Yet despite the limitations of this wartime institution, pacifist women stepped out of the gendered confines of tradition and worked in partnership with men. More than 12,000 men were taking part in a national experiment in which they worked at government-assigned jobs without pay. The gradual and sustained involvement of several thousand pacifist women in this alternative service program—none of them subject to the draft—demonstrates the strong pull of nonconformity for *both* women and men whose family traditions emphasized religious community involvement over political and military participation.

In making choices that went against the broader culture, these pacifists held onto a long-cherished principle of avoiding participation in war. But the roots provided by religious subcultures, so stable in peacetime, were tested in wartime. Increasingly, American conscientious objectors became engaged in secular institutions, drawn by government-sponsored programs like Civilian Public Service that provided opportunities in health care, education, and social service. They hoped to demonstrate that while they were good citizens, they were not, in the phrase of Jean Bethke Elshtain, "wartime civic cheerleaders."

Their deliberate and visible rejection of wartime mobilization reflected inherited traditions of religious pacifism more than concerns about gender equality. Unlike Jane Addams and other American pacifists who in the First World War had staked their claims for women's unique role as peacemakers, and unlike many women of the Vietnam War years who would link peace activism and feminism, the American women who took part in Civilian Public Service made no such assertions. Their actions were infused with ideals of humanitarian service that heralded principles of religious freedom but deemphasized gender. This poses an intriguing contrast to both the commitments of World War I era suffragists who demonstrated against the war and feminists of the Vietnam War era, and it suggests that scholars have yet more work to do in untangling the role of women in the history of conscientious objection during more than two centuries of American warfare.

Conscientious objection has long been considered part of a male domain that encompasses military conscription and duty. Yet it is clear from the varied contributions of women to Civilian Public Service that some American women have appropriated the conscientious objector role as a model for their own lives, even adopting the legal term "conscientious objector" to describe themselves. As Americans commemorate past wars, such as has occurred recently with 50-year retrospectives of the Second World War, women's participation in public and private roles invite broad recognition and historical reevaluation.

Many women practiced restraint in advocating their right to participate in Civilian Public Service; still, they challenged patriarchal church structures and experimented with new ways to meet family obligations, contribute to the labor force, and provide volunteer services. In so doing they stretched the boundaries of conventional gender role expectations. In subsequent decades these formative experiences in *participating* in social change would also shape their expectations of the daughters and sons they would raise.

During World War II American conscientious objectors hoped their humanitarian responses to suffering would stand as a visible counterpoint to the use of massive force even in what the larger society considered to be a "good war." Looking back, many of them believed they had taken the right path; others were less certain that their participation in Civilian Public Service was the most profound statement they could have made against the war. Regardless, their idealism is remarkable in the context of the cultural pressures they faced. Of the lessons to be drawn from their emerging histories, most fundamental is that on the American home front, pluralistic response, not blindly unified assent, characterized civilian life.

Rachel Waltner Goossen teaches history at Goshen [Indiana] College.

Beyond the Blushes
of Song of Songs
by Valerie S. Weaver

Much moves in and out of open windows when our attention is somewhere else.
—Denise Levertov in "Window-Blind"

I never pitied my fifth-grade teacher as much as the day that a defiant classmate insisted on reading out loud from the Song of Songs. Selecting some juicy section like "your navel is a rounded bowl that never lacks mixed wine" or "your two breasts are like fawns," the student proclaimed with glee, "It's in the Bible!" while the rest of us either snickered or blushed. How could something "so naughty" and yet so satisfying to the sexual curiosity of prepubescence come straight from the pages of the Holy Writ?

I'm sure my teacher is not the only who's ever wished that Song of Songs wasn't in the Bible—or at least that it hadn't been dropped into that conspicuous spot between Ecclesiastes and Isaiah. If only it were buried between Nahum and Habakkuk—perhaps then we could better ignore its steamy passion and embarrassingly erotic metaphors.

So sometimes we offer that taming explanation that

the book is an allegory of the relationship between Christ and his bride, the church. Perhaps. But the writer certainly had a lot more fun than he would have needed to describing teeth as "ewes that have come up from the washing" and cheeks "like halves of a pomegranate."

Aside from the sexual nature of Song of Songs that often evokes sophomoric titterings, the book makes us uneasy simply because of its shamelessly tangible images. Its raisins and apples, saffron and henna, turtledoves and gazelles just aren't standard biblical fare. Where are the exhortations, the genealogies, the inspiration? What do we do with such poetry?

It's much the same dilemma the Mennonite church faces with its literary artists. What do we do with these who write with such disrobing honesty and such dazzling disregard for the hallowed idea of "making a point"? What do we do when they write about their sexual lives, their mentally unstable uncles, the eccentric families from the churches of their childhoods? And—horror of all horrors—what do we do when what they write *just isn't true?*

The metaphors, stories, and details that Mennonite poets and novelists offer us are not crafted with the goal of telling-it-exactly-how-it-happened. Those details are gathered by fingers, ears, nose, eyes, and mouths that sense the truths of time and flesh and spirit that run underneath the surface events that the rest of us observe.

While most of us are busy recording minutes at the church business meeting and deciding what color carpet to get for the foyer, the literary artists among us are paying attention to what is moving "in and out of open windows," as Denise Levertov writes. They're tasting phrases like "we are born in a rush of water and cries"; "sometimes these streets hold me as hard as we're held by rich earth"; and "into that space between the three of them . . . fell something cruel and fresh as the sudden air through a window thrown open in a sealed house." By speaking out wordless prayers and yearnings and telling us about the details we never thought mattered, they sharpen our attention to the God of the new wineskins, the unassuming lilies, and the weed-choked seed.

"I have paid attention, and I'm bound to tell what they've seen," writes poet and novelist Walter Wangerin, Jr. Those who tell what they've seen moving through windows and who deem life's sensuous minutia sacred enough to magnify on paper keep us from becoming "culturally insular and spiritually complacent," as Ervin Beck writes. That complacency begins when our senses grow unresponsive to the Spirit and glutted with the abstractions of disembodied religiosity.

The literary artists among us, then, demonstrate sacred attention to the world of details. In the tradition of the writer of Song of Songs, who makes a pure and divine love incarnate in the effusive metaphors of bodies and fruit and spices and rain, they may shock, embarrass, or enthrall us. Like that writer, they also show us the holy delight of paying attention.

Valerie S. Weaver, formerly managing editor of Gospel Herald, *is assistant director of the Lancaster (Pennsylvania) Mediation Center.*

Short Fiction, I

The Fourth Door

a short story

by Sarah Klassen

Jason sits bent forward on a straight-backed chair in the school office, shutting out the conversation meandering between the two secretaries—the one with the straw hair who told him where to sit and the older, grey one. He's reading the last scene of *The Glass Menagerie*, the part where Amanda, the mother, says *Things have a way of turning out so badly.* Jason is not in the habit of evaluating his days, are they good, are they bad. Days come and go and he rarely thinks about his future, which the math teacher, Mr. Melnyk, keeps telling him is spreading out before him like a clean page, or sometimes an open field. Jason would probably see it more as a vague blur, or like smoked glass, opaque.

If Jason were to assess the past week that's come round inevitably to Friday afternoon he would rate it so-so. A new Pink Floyd tape—*Animals*—has been added to his collection. Yesterday the class broke up when he read the part of Tom Wingfield in *The Glass Menagerie*. They cheered and that was cool, not something that happens often to Jason. Wednesday could be written off as a downer because Mrs. Dexter gave him a D for the Macbeth essay, but then he and Blaine skipped Melnyk's math class and biked down the oak-shaded trail along the river and smoked some dope that Blaine brought.

Jason isn't sure why the principal, whom he vaguely despises, has asked to see him. If he wanted to be smart or cynical he could call Hancock senile or just plain stupid, the way he likes to hassle students, but it's hardly worth the effort. He assumes he's been summoned because of skipping math, no big deal. He'll just let Hancock talk and won't say anything, and when the screws tighten he'll mumble that he was depressed about problems at home, personal things he really can't talk about.

It wouldn't be a lie, problems at home. His father absent three years, his mother silent. If his father should ever return, Jason will slam him against the door and kick him down the concrete steps, he will plant his fist in his father's face, he knows he can do it, physically, he's grown. Back then he was bewildered by terror, petrified by his father's huge presence, his rage. Not a drunken rage, Jason can't remember his father drinking. Rather it was an animal rage that found expression in a flesh-on-flesh, bone-on-bone kind of communication. Sometimes there was blood. Jason is quite good at shutting all of it out, shutting out his mother's screams that came muffled through a closed door.

He is nearing the end of the play: *You live in a dream; you manufacture illusions!* Amanda is saying. *Don't let anything interfere with your selfish pleasure! Just go, go, go—to the movies!*

Jason doesn't go to the movies much, but sometimes when school gets tedious he hangs out at K-Mart, the videos and cassettes. The tape decks and CD players.

He has the ability to clear his mind and concentrate on one thing. His huge hands have the amazing skill of moving carefully, stealthily if necessary. He is capable of a certain patience, and, if the occasion requires it, deliberate brutality.

Jason hurries through Amanda's lines, he isn't interested in them, can't imagine a mother who nags like that, his certainly doesn't. He tries not to think too much about his mother, her long silences. Day after day coming home from work at Swift's Packaging, tired. Eats a cheese sandwich or brings a hamburger from MacDonald's. Yesterday he made macaroni and cheese, but she ate very little. Just sat there in the kitchen under the picture of two hands, held vertically and pressed together, praying. The hands have been there as long as Jason can remember. He has no idea whether his mother was praying or not as she rested her head on her weathered, work-worn hand. He doesn't know what he can do for her. It seems to him that she has always been like this, unutterably sad, the house they occupy together pervaded with her sorrow.

He slows down for Tom's lines, rehearsing them noiselessly but with lips moving slightly, maybe Mrs. Dexter will ask him to read Tom's part again, next week. *The more you shout about my selfishness to me the quicker I'll go.* His lips move, he hears Tom's anger in his head. He likes the line. He reads the stage directions: *Tom smashes his glass on the floor. He plunges out the fire escape, slamming the door.* A satisfying kind of excitement, an arousal, moves through his body.

"I hear they had a rock through the front window, and the door kicked in." It's the straw-haired secretary. Her voice, low and languid, intrudes on his reading.

"And about a dozen eggs smashed all over the front. Egg yolk, that's not so easy to clean."

"A shame." The grey secretary.

"Kids are getting so damn violent."

The secretaries seem unaware of Jason who pictures, briefly and with a certain curiosity, egg yolk slithering yellow and thick down the side of a house, sliding over painted wood or filling the roughness of stone or stucco. He returns to Tom's last speech. *The window is filled with pieces of colored glass, tiny transparent bottles in delicate colors, like bits of shattered rainbow.* Jason feels let down by the words. Where's the anger gone, it's anger he's hungry for. He tries to hold on to the excitement, but it diffuses inside him like a wave breaking on sand or like a thinning cloud.

"Jason Flint. In here." The door to the principal's office has opened and Hancock beckons with an authoritative gesture of his close-cropped reddish-blonde head. He is medium in height and slender, the left side of his face scarred with a dull red birthmark, his dark slacks rumpled, his white shirt no longer crisp at the end of the day. He keeps his face deliberately grim.

"Tell me about that Macbeth essay, Jason." He doesn't bother to sit, doesn't ask Jason to sit.

Jason's head jerks up, his shoulders tighten. What does Hancock know about the Macbeth essay? About the D Mrs. Dexter gave him? Jason hasn't forgotten that he demanded a reread, banged his fist hard on her desk, but it seems unimportant now. He's thinking, Macbeth, that can't lead to anything serious. It's Friday and he wants to be out of here.

"To what extent does Macbeth's character determine his tragic downfall." The words slide from his lips automatically, like a recitation, he might be parroting a teacher's assignment, but his voice is innocent of any sarcasm. Then he remembers. "No, no, I mean, it was about the witches, did they influence him or not. Something like that." Jason can't say exactly what the essay was about.

"What mark did you get?"

"D."

"And?"

"And what?"

"Listen, Flint." Hancock is obviously impatient. "You threatened Mrs. Dexter and left the classroom angry. Where did you go?"

"Go?" He's not going to admit he skipped class, not when Hancock hasn't even mentioned Melnyk.

"Let's not play games, Flint. You left school angry Wednesday, went to Mrs. Dexter's house on Kildonan Avenue and for revenge you smashed her window and hurled raw eggs at her house. That's called vandalism, Flint, you got that? Vandalism."

Jason is caught off guard, and for a moment he doesn't know what to say. His silence gives Hancock the hope of victory. He's taken a chance, grabbed a hammer in his groomed right hand, brought it down and hit the nail on the head. Now he raises that hand in nervous relief to his face, as if trying to hide the scar.

As for Jason, he feels suddenly as if he's on fire, his entire body aflame with resentment, his dark brown hair, his purple T-shirt instantly damp. He feels his hands—he is still holding *The Glass Menagerie*—go hard and tight as they instinctively take the balled shape of weapons. In case of a physical encounter between principal and student, Jason would have the advantage: his limbs are young and fierce and every fiber of his body is charged once more with the raw excitement of rage.

The sharp, loud ring of a buzzer proclaims throughout the building that the school week is toast. It is the moment both student and principal have longed for, each in his own way, and the strident signal interrupts the rhythm, the momentum that has been building up in the warm, stale air of the principal's office. Jason can picture all the doors along the hallway opening, students streaming helter-skelter out of classrooms, he can hear a clatter of metal locker doors, an eruption of glad or defiant voices. The stream of color and warm bodies and noise pushes to the doorways and spills into the open air, ejected into the freedom of a June weekend.

More than anything Jason wants to be part of that stream, wants to let it carry him into the street, into its modest possibilities. Right now he wishes for nothing else. As he forces his fists to open, he sees for a moment those other open hands placed carefully together, praying in his mother's kitchen.

"Well you're wrong," he says and he almost adds, "Ask Blaine Schmidt. He was with me," but his brain has signaled "No." What's the point of dragging in Blaine and the dope, he can't do that to Blaine. His loyalty surprises him. It was just a fluke, skipping class with Blaine, they aren't really friends, had spoken very little there beside the river.

"Phone my mother," he says, and this too surprises him. How could she possibly help him, his silent mother?

"The number, Flint?" Hancock's hand has already lifted the receiver, his index finger is poised to dial.

It's possible, because it's Friday, that his mother will actually be home from work. She comes in the door and the phone rings, she dumps her worn cloth handbag on a chair and moves wearily to pick up the receiver. "Hello." Her voice is faint and wooden and so crammed with exhaustion Jason feels compelled to shield her.

"Actually, no, my mom isn't home," he says, quickly, thinking, what can I say now, what will work? God, how can I keep her out of this. "I didn't do it, Mr. Hancock, I swear to God I wasn't anywhere near Kildonan Street Wednesday." His passion, earnest and almost desperate, surprises him. It also surprises Hancock.

"Go on." Hancock sits and motions Jason to a chair. The receiver is back in its cradle. Has the hammer, after all, not hit the nail on the head?

A shaft of light pours through the narrow window. What a jail this room is, Jason thinks, what a bloody jail. He catches a faint glimmer of the irony that Hancock too passes the days in a prison cell. But now is the time to hint about the problems at home, imply unspeakable things without giving anything away, without dragging his mother too far into this. He can't seem to begin, the noise in the hallway is already diminishing, the building is being emptied out and to keep sitting here in this alien place with a man who is a stranger is unbearable and ludicrous.

"Actually my mother's out of town for the weekend," Jason says, shaping the words slowly, deliberately. "She needed a break, she's . . ." he stops himself, wondering who there is in the whole world to trust, can anyone ever be counted on? Jason is bent forward in the chair, elbows on knees, his forearms vertical, hands pressed together with *The Glass Menagerie* gripped between them, the fingertips almost touching his chin. His slumped shoulders feel tight as a tightly wound steel spring. "I'll tell her when she comes back, she can phone you Monday, or better Tuesday." How much does he dare stretch the time?

"I didn't do it," he says again. "Okay, maybe I was rude to her but I didn't smash her window." His voice is becoming calm, the rage is there inside him, but he can handle it. By Tuesday, who knows, something will turn up. He looks up, looks at Hancock who isn't looking at him but into the distance somewhere above the closed door.

Hancock has lost interest, lost that firmness of purpose he had when he opened his office door and motioned with a confident gesture of his head for Jason Flint to enter. Is he thinking Jason is probably lying about his mother, and what sounds like sincerity is really fake? He's no longer certain. It takes an effort of will to refrain from looking at his wristwatch.

"Why can't you kids for once think of the bigger picture. I can't run a school without rules. Society can't be a decent place unless everyone works together." The hint of whining in Hancock's voice rouses in Jason a faint flicker of contempt. He knows now there will be no phone call home and no detention. Not today. And along with the contempt and the knowing comes a glimmer of gratitude.

Jason runs a finger aimlessly along the polished wood behind a row of books on the principal's desk. The finger picks up dust. On the other side of the door there is a scraping of chairs, a blur of voices, the secretaries are getting ready to leave.

Only a few students are still at the bus stop when Jason walks out into the street, into the warm June afternoon, trying to shake off the trapped feeling, the foreignness that inhabits the hallways and classrooms where he spends so many hours each week. He doesn't speak to anyone at the bus stop, cuts through the K-Mart parking lot where he slows his stride, thinking maybe this is a place he could hang out for a while. But he continues walking, neither in a hurry nor hesitant, and comes eventually to the low-rental housing where he lives, behind the fourth door, with his mother. Two or three children are playing near the large garbage bin. A woman is collecting toys from the steps, a red plastic airplane, a doll, a couple of dinosaurs. In this place Hancock does not exist, nor Mrs. Dexter, nor the two secretaries, nor Macbeth, though if Jason wanted to, he could imagine Tom Wingfield approaching or moving away from such a door as this, cradling his desires the way a mother might cradle a child, with fear and doubt and love.

Jason is aware of being hungry as he climbs the wooden steps, but he doesn't comfort himself with the vain hope that his mother is planning fried chicken for supper. He thinks he should go next door to borrow a lawn mower and cut the small patch of grass that's going to seed in front of their unit. But the sun is still high and hot and he doesn't feel like it. His hands are relaxed now. One of them still holds his copy of *The Glass Menagerie.*

"Take it easy, Flint," Hancock said when he finally held the door open. "If your mother's away, just make sure she doesn't come home to . . ." As he groped for something to say he let his eyes meet Jason's and

Jason saw that they were blue and held a glint of curiosity.

"Just give her a break, Jason."

Fumbling for his key, Jason knows with jolting certainty that this weekend Hancock's dull red scar and the curiosity in his blue eyes will accompany him, relentlessly, as he goes in and out through this door. And at night, when Jason closes his eyes for sleep, they will still be there in the darkness.

Sarah Klassen is a poet and short story writer who lives in Winnipeg, Manitoba.

By the Editors

Guerrillas in Community
by Phyllis Pellman Good

It may seem like a mismatch—Mennonites stewing about wielding power and authority. Yet our move into the professions, our incessant forming of institutions, and our long history of creating businesses put us in the middle of these subjects, whether we like it or not.

These are matters many of us would prefer to duck—and many of us have tried—but they are overdue for a frontal airing.

Power and authority are unnerving issues for almost any North American at the end of the 20th century. Place a bunch of Mennonites in this milieu of horror about authority—jacked up by our own peculiar memories of it, as well as our historical uneasiness about power—and you have a situation that can turn vibrantly skittish.

Let me begin with a few hunches. In short, North American Mennonites are wary of authoritarianism, or the possible misuse of authority. We grant that authority is necessary, although we are mightily concerned about where it is lodged and how it is exercised.

On the other hand, we seem to have warmed up to the matter of power. Maybe because more of us have more of it. We have felt it in our fingers. We have begun to believe it may be an inevitable part of our world, so we seem less apt to deny it or disparage it. (Humility, on the other hand, although once revered, seems to have fallen out of favor.)

I offer this backdrop of hunches as a way to describe a possible common mind among us. I also must mention a caveat and make a confession: I don't bring answers. I do bring observations, questions, and wishes.

First, some observations.

Most of us have not kept our practice of a faith community up-to-date with the rest of our lives. Our thinking and our theology lag behind our living these days.

The agrarian neighborhoods we once knew were good soil for our faith communities. We regularly drove by each other's homes, saw each other in the hardware and grocery stores, shared equipment, made chow-chow together, prayed and sang side-by-side at Wednesday evening prayer meeting and Sunday morning and evening church services. Interchange was constant and natural. Authority lay within the faith community, bouyed up by our parallel lives and our intimate knowledge of what we each did day-to-day.

Many of us carry the memory of the communal authority and power that was residual in that faith-life world. But now most of us live two-track lives—our career or business life, and our church life—two worlds essentially separate from each other, unless we individually choose to bring them together. It's our choice if it happens. And then we individually set the conditions. Such a set-up obviously vests very little real power or authority within the church body.

And yet we have this sort of yearning. We wish our faith could not only inform our lives, but could also fundamentally shape our living. And so we make attempts to fit in and belong to a congregation, even if we aren't prepared to yield it control over our lives. In my congregation, for example, the business persons, the bankers, and the professionals mostly dress down on a Sunday morning. We bring our casseroles to the fellowship meals. We show up at the extra events, often coming late and leaving early, but we make a real effort to be there. We keep a social toehold in the congregation, we give our offerings there, we actually worship on those benches, but, for the most part, we hold our business projects, our fiscal strategies, our troubling dilemmas, very tightly to ourselves.

In fact, the persons who know us best, and from whom we seek counsel, are likely to be our colleagues, who understand our business or professional world and who are not shocked by what we live with. They may not share the fine-tuning of our morals or have the same commitments, but they know our lives. When we ask their opinion, when we go to them for advice, we throw authority to them. They have earned it, we sense. Their knowledge and experience give them credence and power.

How, I wonder, does the church garner authority in situations where it knows little? Where it has had little experience?

And so, I realize, we increasingly find authority outside our faith community.

A second observation. The church tends to be

impressed with its members who are financially successful, those who have educational stature, and those who hold prestigious professional occupations. The church may also be uncomfortable with the same.

How it treats its members who fit any of the above categories varies from being deferential to being highly critical. We in the church seem to find it difficult to set aside the sort of carnal respect the larger world doles out to its well endowed members. Too often our measuring sticks are skewed and we become confused about what the standards should be.

We are intimidated by the power of money or knowledge or prestige—to the detriment of all involved. Community gives way to strata.

I have seen two patterns. In one, the person of wealth (whatever its currency—money, degrees, experience, positions) is assumed to be wise in all subjects and to be capable in all positions. We grant her churchly authority because she is a professional "expert." I have been told of one congregation in which such person attends only the Sunday morning worship hour (and perhaps only half of those), frequently goes to work in her office while her family attends Sunday School, occasionally agrees to take a position of responsibility within the congregation but almost never finds time to do the work it requires, and yet is repeatedly asked for advice and to give an opinion at certain critical moments. "Accountability," a pet Mennonite ideal, seems not to matter in this case.

In another situation, a business person who faced some difficulty was suddenly under attack by church leadership. Latent resentment for the power this person had held in the church and community seemed to be at play when the congregational leaders' response was compared to the way they had handled other thorny issues—a messy divorce and a prospective member who questioned the need to be baptized. This time the standard of Accountability was brought out and wielded like a sledgehammer. "Maybe I embarrassed them," reflected the subject of their pursuit. "Or maybe I was seen as a test case. They were going to use the church's authority to punish me, and they came after me guerrilla-style, making broad innuendoes about my business activity and seeming to discredit my integrity."

Either behavior is distorted—either illegitimately granting too much power to the powerful, or setting a higher standard for the powerful than is exacted of "ordinary" members. Faced with "powerful" members, all of us—and perhaps especially those in positions of leadership in the church—often become confused about our own practice of authority and power.

Observation three. We seem to have far less pause about exercising our power in our business and professional worlds than we do in the church. Many of us accept the understanding that if we have it career-wise, we bear the responsibility to use it.

Some of us develop two styles—to match our divided worlds. We pull forward all of our imagination, our training, our lessons learned from living, and go headlong into the professional fray. Our businesses demand much, and we give all we can. It is a tough, unbuffered world, and we meet it.

Not overshooting at church, then, can be a real trick. And figuring out what the rules are for operating in a community of shared faith and mutual submission is a huge cloud of a question, especially for those of us who have every nerve on alert in our careers, who fine-tune our strategies and monitor our competitors as naturally as we breathe. How are we supposed to behave in church? How are we full members of a faith community that asks us to be honest, and yet yielding to each other?

Some of us leave our Mennonite congregations because we can't figure it out, or it takes too much energy, or we're tired of the subtle judgment. For years, in our community, we've watched successful business persons drift over to a church that seems more accepting, or doesn't ask as much, or maybe doesn't "imply" as much as we Mennonites do, with our long and tenacious memories and ideals of living simply, meekly, and humbly.

Some of us stay, but grow ever more polite and distant within our congregations. We've accepted that we are all "specialists" of sorts, without the right to comment on, or have opinions about, each other's lives. We simply don't have enough information about each other's worlds, we believe. We may share a pew, but that is the extent of our common territory.

Others of us wish for company in an effort that would require much of all who agree to be part of it. The intent would be this—to willingly and deliberately find a faith community to which I can fully belong—me and my peculiarities and my weaknesses—and my assets.

Would it be possible to offer this sort of sanctuary and accountability to each other? Would it work to grant authority and power to a group of fellow seekers, in a move both to discipline and cultivate our personal holdings of assets, whatever their form—money, degrees, titles, positions?

It is a strenuous exercise to insist that these two primary parts of one's life overlap. It is not natural in this world to have one's faith overlay one's business or academic or professional life. Such an effort will result in tension. It risks misunderstanding. It does require persistent intention to have each sphere inform and shape the other.

None of us, I believe, can manage such an effort alone. If we want it, we must each choose to live an "observed" life. Then the question becomes, can I find others who will join in this commitment to an active faith-life, to holding all this in balance? Without it, we will go on leading our fragmented, disjointed lives. Given our times, given our own particular church history, given our deep and prosperous investment in business and the professions, this granting of power and authority to some form of church will happen only if each one of us initiates it, only if we each see to it, only if we each submit to it.

Otherwise we go on behaving like guerrillas in community, holding our private secrets while singing out our well-advertised theologies of how it ought to be. We are tempted to send out missiles that cloud or discredit those who seem to have too much power or authority or credence. We tolerate but seldom respect our well-meaning, but relatively insulated, congregational and church agency leaders, who can seem primarily concerned that nothing "un-toward" happens, who hope not to witness a flat-out debate, or even a shouting match, about how faith and life might appropriately go hand-in-hand.

It takes courage to handle power. It takes equal courage to deliberately yield power. If we can—if we dare—we can return authority to each other within the faith community. And have powerful company on the way.

Phyllis Pellman Good, Lancaster, Pennsylvania, is a writer, editor, and co-editor of this collection.

Affluence and Edfluence
by Merle Good

One of the most effective arguments to belittle concerns about Affluence is to ask where "conscientious living" ends and Affluence begins. Should one own a home? Should one always drive a used car? Or is living below your means an inverse sense of pride? Who in the church can say how much is too much?

To me, Affluence means placing too much value on material things. Whether we have dozens or millions may not be the deciding factor—it's our attitude toward these things—and how that shapes our understanding of who we are, and how important we think we are.

Affluence affects our self-image. That corrosive seduction of the spirit can make any one of us into a callous, self-centered snob, whether we possess many or few material goods. It's what Affluence does to our head that makes it so dangerous.

The same can be true of Edfluence. I define Edfluence as placing too much value on formal learning and on securing degrees. This description may seem difficult to grasp for some, especially for those persons who have advanced degrees. Many educated persons deny that they suffer from Edfluence—and emphatically argue that formal education is always good because it liberates and broadens persons.

But persons who have placed less capital in formal education often find it easy to spot Edfluence. They see that same corrosive seduction of the spirit. And as with Affluence, it's what Edfluence does to our heads that makes it so dangerous. The debate is less about how much formal education one should possess than it is about attitude—how does it affect our self-image?

Many academics assert that they live simply and have few possessions. But others may observe their wealth in their heavy investment in formal schooling to secure degrees. Those degrees, along with resumes and published articles and books, represent as potent a holding of "capital" as a small business person may have in his or her retail store or manufacturing shop.

Business entrepreneurs and academic entrepreneurs are often very similar in their outlook and motivation. But the church has tended to chide only the business persons (even while soliciting donation dollars from them to shore up flagging institutions). This results in the academics assuming their motives and their work are more pure. Furthermore, many in the church seem to have decided it would be impolite to witness against the Edfluence of their members.

Both types of entrepreneurs have capital (possessions). Both use language and structure to exclude the majority while keeping their own positions safely established. Both tend to live in segregated neighborhoods (ie., an upper class community for executives or a university-style neighborhood). And both risk the danger of thinking God and others may not be as important as some say.

But Affluence and Edfluence are not attitudes which

are limited to those with ambition and drive. Some of the rest of us may face their seductive powers, too.

Perhaps we should learn to ask ourselves—Why do I want this thing? Whether it's a new house or a new degree, *why* do I want it? Why am I so impressed with this thing in others? What are my motives?

We've heard a lot through the years about the hypocritical nature of motives. "We need a bigger house so we can have more guests from church." (Read—we want a bigger house and we'll try to justify it by saying we'll be more devout.) Likewise with degrees. "I think this degree will help me to serve humankind better." (Read—I'll make a better income.)

Or take that illusive ideal of becoming a "broadened" person. The affluent may say they travel a lot to become more exposed. Could be. It also puts them in the upper class. Likewise, one of the great justifications of the edfluent is that their investment broadens their worldview. Could be, also. But it also places them in the intellectual elite where supposedly fewer persons will look down on them.

Why are we tempted to accumulate? Why is it so important to us to feel superior to others?

How many small groups question one of their members who's thinking of pursuing a college or graduate degree? Rather than assume automatically that "it's a good thing, if you can afford it," aren't there questions which might prove helpful in the Christian walk? (Of course, many small groups may have ceased long ago to quiz members who are buying new cars and gadgets, moving to better neighborhoods, or accumulating stocks and bonds.)

Which leads us to another question—is there more

preaching in Mennonite circles against Affluence than against Edfluence?

My observation is that the more education Pastor A has, the less likely Pastor A is to raise concerns about Edfluence. And the reverse tends to be true—the more closely Pastor B is tied to wealthy families and members, the less likely Pastor B is to raise concerns about Affluence.

But there's another wrinkle—Pastor A, while winking at Edfluence, will probably be willing to speak out against Affluence. But Pastor B will probably not risk a critique of either Affluence or Edfluence.

This is all complicated by the fact that the church is in the education business. Our denomination owns colleges and seminaries. All members are encouraged to think of themselves as stockholders. Therefore, to be a good company person, one does not raise concerns which may undercut those educational institutions which the church owns and operates. (Imagine what would have happened to the *More-with-Less Cookbook* if the denomination had owned a series of upscale restaurants!)

I believe Edfluence can be as much of a seduction at one of our church schools as at a state university—just as Affluence can be a temptation whether one works for a Mennonite employer or for a company owned by non-Christians.

It all boils down to this: What does our accumulation of formal learning or of material goods do to our heads?

Which brings me to my final prayer. I covet for myself and my generation—and for our children—two qualities which seem out of style these days: wisdom and humility.

What is wisdom? Isn't it the same as learning? Actually, wisdom and learning are really quite different. Learning is easily gotten, but it generally does not lead to wisdom.

I did a lot of thinking about wisdom and humility during my three years in an Ivy League seminary two decades ago. And I've come to think that perhaps wisdom was no more present among the educated elite than among the common folk. Perhaps less so. Wisdom comes from a certain humility before God and other human beings, and that's an experience which eludes many who possess a wealth of learning or a wealth of material goods.

Is it possible that the more we accumulate, the more narrow we become? Sometimes it seems that persons with lots of material goods tend to regard most of God's humankind as peasants, and persons with lots of academic goods tend to regard most of the rest of the world as intellectual peons. (There are many exceptions, of course.)

Is it a given that the higher the income, the lower the esteem for other folk; the bigger the university degree, the smaller and more narrow-minded the attitude toward others? "More" often handicaps persons; "seeking more" blinds us to our own shallow smallness.

This is not to suggest that an humble Christian with the gift of wisdom will have no possessions and no formal learning. But we must recognize the seductive power of these forces to dull our hearts and minds to the work of God in our lives and in others.

If Affluence and Edfluence determine who's in and who's out, who may speak and who may decide, and even how we define who we are, wisdom and humility will long ago have disappeared to other hearts more open to the voice of God.

Merle Good of Lancaster, Pennsylvania, is a writer, dramatist, publisher, and a co-editor of this volume.

Poetry, I

Driving West on Easter
by Jeff Gundy

1.

What does it take to make the trip? I would settle for
the voice of God, a sign, a note. The sign I have says
route 30, Buettner Road. On a white barn, shadow
cutouts, waving man and woman, jumping dog, cheerful as television. Three thin girls in Wolcott, walking,
smoking, smiling. Me in my white car, unobserved,
wanting every leaf to be a bird, every bird an angel.
Something in the ditch—a dingy paper, filled with
wind.

2.

A man needs to dream, even if it's hard as passing on
route 24, risky as writing in this notebook propped on
the steering wheel, the jerk of adrenalin as tons of
metal loom inches from my cherished flesh. Stupid, I
know, but what would you do, the absolute quick hum
leaks in at every seam, the final whisper drums in the
winds of passage, the engine murmurs now, now. On
the overpass: I love you Jeff. Just like that.

3.

South of Gridley, a quarter-section remnant of prairie, charred yesterday by a sweaty white-haired man whose picture made the paper, dragging a fire broom, spreading flames, hurrying carefully, explaining the centuries of practice on his side. I love that picture, I want to drag a fire broom over my prairies, run beside the clean flames, watch the dainty shoots sniff into the sunlight. But here the smoke has cleared, it's a blue still Easter in the Mackinaw Breaks, yellow branches, red branches, making their beautiful empty moves.

4.

Two hours 46 minutes to St. Louis, the bridge over the strong brown god. I sweep down a long hill into the Loutre River valley, buds swelling, nets of yellow, green, red, caught in the small trees. How big the world is. How hard to keep it in my head.

5.

And I know what binds me, sends me cruising toward Emporia on new blacktop, the swerves and maneuvers that have me driving west on Easter to say my songs for strangers. No simple life. No blazing sign. Moments when the traffic thins, the road arrows to the west, the sun makes another run on the warm skin of the world. These words, just rehearsals for the great day when the glowing vowels will stretch from cup to wine, from chapter to verse, all along the roaring stone and flesh and wind and fire that is me and you and the Mongol hordes and the secret lives in the Marianas Trench, the world that climbs and spins in the Kansas evening, calm and still and moving as Easter in a car alone, six hundred miles behind me and a dozen to go, twelve miles to Newton and the house of the stranger who asked me to come, so far, so good, where the guest room is ready when I knock on the door.

Jeff Gundy is a poet and English professor at Bluffton (Ohio) College.

On This Earth

by *Juanita Brunk*

To love my own, my body,
to know without saying, *Legs, you are good legs,*
and feet and stomach and arms, good, and the spaces
under my arms, and the brown pigments
splashed across my back like tea leaves.
To love my body the way
I sometimes love a stranger's: a woman
on the subway, tired, holding her two bags,
a child slumped against her like another sack
as the train stops and starts and the child
   says something
so quietly no one else can hear it,
but she leans down, and whispers back,
and the child curls closer. I would love my body
the way a mother can love her child, or the way
a child will love anyone
who gives it a home on this earth, a place
without which it would be nothing, a dry branch
at the window of a lit room.

Juanita Brunk is a poet who lives in Brooklyn, New York.

Rough-Cut Head
by Keith Ratzlaff

after Paul Klee

When the woman in the purple trousers
on the bicycle—now at the corner
now up the street by the sign
now by the tree—turned the corner,
I thought of her in the dual wind:
the cold one from the west today—
and the other wind beginning with her
spreading out behind her like geese.
I thought about her flying hair
and the cowl of her skin
and her forehead
defined and reddened by the wind,
of her lips defined and burnished
by the wind. And how even on a bicycle,
how easily we breathe and how easily
our wondrous heads are invaded by the wind.

How open and hollow are the mouth's courtyard,
or the sinuses, or the hallways of the ear.
How vulnerable. How much of us is absence
like drawers, or pictures of absence—
the sky in the photos of clouds at night,
the outline of a breast in an x-ray

taken before the mastectomy.
How easy it is to find a place in the skull
for the chisel, or the gun, or the wind
and its glitter. We are alterable.

I know a plastic surgeon who put the gun
in his mouth, fired, and lived.
Think of the echo. The brain in its great hall
banquetting, then besieged. And the joy of impact—
the eyes unbolted, shifting, siting new stars
in the new red sky, the jaw turned to grit
and glitter the wind would fling at us later.
He was depressed for reasons he couldn't name.
In woodshop he has made a letterholder
covered in curious purple spangles.

Keith Ratzlaff is a poet and teaches at Central College,
Pella, Iowa.

The Tragedy
by Kate Good

with gratitude to Picasso

Three figures stand on the shore,
once a family,
now more alone together,
washed in a deeper blue than the water or sky
that holds them up. Side by side in their need for
one moment—
a memorial of stillness when everything stops.
A brief break in the eternal successful
crash of the waves, the laugh and dance
of the gull, the lively breath of air. Then all that
will live and grow in that empty vacuum
is their loss
with its bellow echoing again and again in their
heads, rocking their bodies with its force.
They know the peace of uninterrupted
pain will never come.

If the world stopped for one
tragedy, it would never begin again.
So all that is left to do is protect
their hearts with their arms.
As if each winding and holding their limbs,

flesh rubbing against muscle and bone,
could piece the fragments of their being together again.

*Kate Good is a student at Eastern Mennonite University,
Harrisonburg, Virginia.*

The Water Table, There It Is

by Janet Kauffman

The water table, there it is, although there is no fire
floor or earth bed, not yet. Here's an air mattress.
Won't you lie down? The water table lies, or stands,
under the field, and it can be a surprise
how close to the surface the table (never set,
it's heaped) is buried, sometimes a plow-bade's
depth, the metal scrapes water and the tractor sways
on floating ground where crayfish have built up
gray chunk chimneys. Apartments are mortared,
cellars sink and fill with duckweed and water plaintain.
Are you rested? How long did you sleep? You can
put your elbows on the table. It is floral and amoral
and porous to the elements, the touch of anything.

*Janet Kauffman is a novelist who lives in Hudson,
Michigan.*

For Trudy, My Aunt
by Barbara Nickel

August 4, 1931
Great Deer, Saskatchewan

My grandma makes a poultice for your chest:
mustard, rags, flour against a wheeze and cough
incessant as the dust. She wants to rest,
your lips chapped creek beds bluing behind the rough
fence of your crib. Grandpa's decreed, "Doctor's
too far, no sense." Across the yard his feed pails
jangle, dull bells tripped by the wind. He's poured
years into fields. The wheat will fail and fail.
It's hot. The third night—Grandma falls asleep
and dreams you pick blue harebells near the slough,
you have new breasts, barn cats spill from your lap,
you smell like rain. She wakes. Fever's killed you.
She takes you out to rock until the sky
is filled with thunder clouds in your blue eyes.

Barbara Nickel is a poet and teacher at the University of
British Columbia in Vancouver.

Ceremony
by Raylene Hinz-Penner

This country's greatest living Peace Chief among the
    Cheyenne is burying
my Aunt Ruth in the corner of Bergthal Cemetery on
    a red dirt road
that will take you back south into town, into Corn,
    Oklahoma.

We stand on ground my great-grandfather Julius took,
    horseback
in the run on the Territories. Most of the stones bear
    my family name.
Now, the names of uncles and aunts. My cousin tells
    me how she came here

last year with her father, before he died, to bury his
    old cousin, how,
as the procession mounted the hill, they found the
    dead man's beautiful horse
standing at attention above his grave. At the end, it
    was the horse he loved best.

The Reverend Lawrence Hart, Cheyenne Chief and
    Mennonite minister, gathers us
around her. His flat straight hand points like an arrow
    to the sky, a pose

I know from pictures in history books. His voice is
    deep and solemn,

the voice I imagine, used also by his father before him
    who my mother says
came here often to preach in our church, vacant and
    unceremonious now:
The Lord giveth and the Lord taketh away; blessed be the
name of the Lord.

What we have left are words we have agreed to share.
    We bring them back
here from only half-remembered pasts to believe
    them again, grab at them anew
to take them home and test them on our lived lives.
    Our history now, the crazy

spinning of a thousand stories we love into earth's
    silence, into forgetfulness,
we hang on tight to the phrase, erect it with wonder
    in the open air
like a structure on a new frontier, as if we could walk
    inside it and worship.

Raylene Hinz-Penner is a poet and lives in Newton,
Kansas.

In Ascension Day's Wake
by Regina Weaver

When the young woman arrived
at the church that morning,
she saw familiar faces,
many from her youth,
and thought how beautiful they were
joining together
in honor of a person's life.
Why couldn't every day be
as steeped in shared emotion?

Later, when she spoke about it
on the phone to her mother,
she learned the man had died
on Ascension Day, high noon.
It moved her to imagine
his spirit soaring
from his body at the hour
when he'd cast no shadow.

At the church she'd sensed him flying
back and forth above their heads
skimming the brows of friends, the hair
of children. She'd felt
then, how difficult it must be

for him to leave all this,
his sorrow and his joy in the air
above them.

Regina Weaver is a writer living in Seattle, Washington.

Featured Articles, Essays, and Opinions, II

Excelsior

by Warren Kliewer

Children are always having to look up, because everyone else is bigger and taller. All the interesting stuff is out of reach: cookies, colored glass, knives, matches. I remember thinking: "Someday I'll get big and then I'll find out what's on top of things."

We've all gone through that childhood discomfiture, of course, and that may be the origin of judgmental idioms like "to look down on" someone. "Oh, isn't he the cutest little boy," some strange lady would coo, looking down at the top of my head.

"You wait till I get big like you," I'd say to myself. "I'll show you what cute is."

Maybe the opposite idiom, "to look up to," also comes from starting out life as a miniature. I know I looked up to (in both senses) the boys next door, not only because Allen was one year and two inches beyond me, but because of the splendid things he did. Wisecracks. Funny words that made me laugh till my stomach hurt. Wherever he went, other boys gathered around to ask him dumb questions for his funny answers. The cartoons he drew in class made even the teachers laugh. All I could do was tell solemn stories; Allen could make anything funny.

His brother, Lee, 11 years older than I, was a mystery beyond emulation, an idol surrounded by magic. I was five and hung back three steps when I followed him. I had to strain my neck back to look all the way up to his face, and was glad to do it.

One day another boy in the neighborhood raced past our front yard shouting, "It's here! It came!"

"What? What came? Where is it?"

"On their front porch."

So I followed. There, behind the thick, white railings and broad, tapered columns, the thing was . . . whatever it was. A large, wooden packing crate, partly opened. A few shiny metal cylinders and poles scattered around the porch floor. Some polished, brown wooden bars lined up against the wall.

"What is it?"

"Sh," someone said. "Just wait."

All these mysterious things had been packed in the crate in what looked like straw, only it really wasn't. "What's that stuff?"

That was the day I learned the word, "excelsior." It's not just straw, I learned, not just wood shavings. This was a word my mouth could play with, my mind could mull over: Excelsior! Ex-CEL-si-or.

Thick rubber wheels came out of the box, each one wrapped in padded paper and tied with twine.

"What are those for?"

"You'll see."

Nobody was explaining anything. Then I saw a pattern. As the shiny metal tubes in different lengths, two of each length, came out of the crate, Lee laid them gently in pairs in a row against the wall. "What are those for?"

"Resonance," Lee answered authoritatively. "And

amplification." Oh, I was seized with admiration all over again. To be able to say such meaningless things with such assurance! I didn't ask what the words meant.

My mother called me for dinner, had to call twice, in fact, I was so engrossed. Since being late for meals was an unpardonable offense, I kicked my way through the hedge rather than going around it, frustrated because I still had no idea what those pipes and blocks would become. I asked my mother if she knew.

"A marimba," she said casually.

That was no help. Knowing the name of a thing didn't tell me what it did. "What's a marimba?"

"You'll see," my father said. "Eat your dinner."

And then I had to take my nap, and, by the time I got back to Lee's porch, the pipes and blocks and wheels had been moved into the house, and nothing was left but the packing crate and the excelsior. So I peeked through the window and couldn't see anything, but I heard sounds from the second floor, and I couldn't go in because no one had invited me, so I knew I was never going to find out ever in my entire life what a marimba was.

But I was five years old and easily distracted. A week or two later Mr. Sorensen dropped in. He roamed throughout the country peddling Watkins Products, carrying along a heavy valise packed with shoe polish and vanilla and cinnamon and greasy ointments and, of course, liniment. Wherever he went, he trailed the smell of liniment, and it lingered for an hour after he'd left. It filled the room. So did his voice, sounding always as if on the verge of roars of laughter. Mr.

Sorensen was fat. No, he was immense, his face, his calves, even his fingers. I knew what Santa Claus looked like. He was Mr. Sorensen. Though he lacked a beard, he had the belly, and, when he laughed, it really did shake like a bowlful of jelly.

Mr. Sorensen's visits were conducted like a ritual. He would drop in. No one made appointments in those days. He'd head straight for a kitchen chair, plop down, and catch his breath. Then he'd begin talking—about the weather, the crops, the local news, somebody's new baby, no politics or gossip—and casually, as if it were of no importance, he'd open a whole side of the valise and reveal a densely packed display of brightly colored bottles, tins, boxes, and paper packages. And in the middle of a very interesting story, he'd interrupt himself to say, "You see anything here you need, Mrs. Kliewer?"

"No," my mother would say. Her sales resistance was formidable. The year was 1936, and even pennies were scarce. She smiled.

And without a break in his rhythm, he'd continue his story and take one bottle or box after another out of his valise and arrange the items tastefully on the kitchen table, and he'd start a new story about a friend or relative or customer at the other end of the county and unpack and arrange a few more tins and paper packages and interrupt himself with, "Anything here? This is a good salve for bee stings."

Every once in a while my mother would cave in. She'd pick up one item, only one, set it aside, go quickly into the bedroom for the little coin purse inside her large purse, and come back with exact change. As Mr. Sorensen repacked, she'd offer him coffee or something to eat—apple pie, if he came early in the week. Then if I'd been listening hard and encouraging him, he'd lean back in the kitchen chair and tell me stories about the Old Country, Denmark.

Even though I was a five-year-old who had never heard of Hans Christian Andersen and wouldn't learn about ancient Scandinavian storytelling traditions for another 20 or more years, I knew a performance when I saw one. He was a part-time bard with a kitchen chair for dais, performing for an awe-stricken audience of one.

In those days performance permeated our lives, though we would have been shocked if anyone had pointed it out that bluntly. No, the church choir sang every Sunday, not "performed." Children memorized Bible verses in Sunday school and then recited them, not "performed." Businessmen gave speeches in the Commercial Club meetings (when Rotary had not yet arrived), and teachers told well-rehearsed stories to their classes, and we all knew them to be fine, upstanding citizens, not like the wicked men and loose women who worked on the stage. And yet, in those days before television, when radios were rarely used, we were being taught the rhythm of performance: private study followed by the public projection of a controlled persona. When I judged Mr. Sorensen to be a master storyteller, I already had criteria by which to measure him.

So I was doubly amazed when I finally saw and heard the assembled marimba—the pipe legs so shiny you could see an elongated reflection of your face on them, hanging down in graduated rows like organ pipes upside down, the burnished, brown blocks of wood laid out neatly, the longest on the left tapering down to the shortest on the right. I wanted to touch it but didn't dare, or, more likely, Lee told me not to. Then he played, using two sets of the round-headed mallets, one hard and one padded with fuzzy coverings. The music swelled to fill the sitting room with marimba throbs and then dwindled down to a whisper my ears could hardly pick up. The little mallets moved so fast they blurred. "Mama," I said when I got home, "Lee is a genius."

She stopped working at the kitchen table. "Where did you learn that word?"

"From Lee."

She smiled. "All right."

Years later, of course, after I'd come to understand how things work, I realized Lee hadn't learned to play the marimba magically overnight. Besides, this was 1936. No one, certainly not Lee's father, the vice-president of the Farmers State Bank, was risking money on a cumbersome toy before his son had demonstrated his commitment. No, I realized, Lee had learned on a borrowed instrument somewhere, under the thumb of a teacher, through relentless practice and drudgery, just like any other musician.

But starting out in ignorance, believing Lee was a wizard, was still the better way. For now I have the memory of the magic, and it resurfaces from time to time to remind me that a fine performance really is a mystery after all. Performers, at least the ones who reach beyond technique, find themselves floating into a region even they do not understand, and, when they return, they're not able to describe that alien geography. This uncharted somewhere: is this what Longfellow had in mind when he imposed another meaning on the word "excelsior" in one of his poems—a yearning upwards toward higher things? His usage, which I am told is ungrammatical Latin, was suitably unspecific.

I learned about yearning—the experience if not the word—the next summer when I turned six. Someone told me there was going to be a show in town. I didn't dare ask what a show is because everyone else acted as if they knew. I did know what a stage is. Our school auditorium had one—a plain, dark-brown proscenium with realistically painted foliage and marble pedestals on a wing-and-drop set. If that's where the show was to be, I knew I could go. There was only one house and an alley between us and the auditorium, so I could go there any time I wanted.

But I guessed wrong. The show was going to be in Balzer's Lumber Yard. I couldn't go! My mother would never allow me to cross the traffic on Highway 60, not on a Saturday afternoon when there were so many cars out there. Then one of the other boys mentioned tickets. Was I going to have to pay? I didn't have any money. I was just a little kid. Would anyone really expect a little kid to pay? I knew I was going to have to enlist my mother's aid.

I think she was curious about the show herself. That's why I didn't have to beg. Early Saturday morning she raided her little coin purse inside her big purse, and we set off. "There's plenty of time," she told me when I tried to get her to walk faster.

Balzer's Lumber Yard had a driveway through the center of the building so that trucks could load and unload during the winters or when it rained. Everything had been cleard out now, and many rows of metal folding chairs had been set up, all facing a stage. Only it was too small for people to walk around on.

"How come?" I asked my mother.

"It's a puppet show," she said.

"What's a puppet?"

"It's like a doll, but it moves."

"It moves? How?"

"You'll see." People were always telling me that.

I rushed to get a seat in the front row—easy enough, since most of the chairs were still empty, except for a few other boys who had squabbled for the best seats. They tried to talk to me, but I couldn't think of anything to say, now when something so mysterious was about to happen. I turned my eyes to the stage. It was so high up I had to arch my neck backwards to look at it. The curtain was closed. Nothing moved. I studied it.

The mothers, I think, gathered in the back, but I forgot there were mothers anywhere in the world. More and more children came in and sat down. I stared at the stage curtains, hoping that if I wished hard enough, they would open. They didn't. The chairs were all full. The other children grew noisier. I was no longer able to make a sound. Maybe someone should go behind the curtains and tell the puppets we were all ready. No one did. My muscles ached. My breathing sped up.

Then the curtains opened. Bright light flooded the little stage. From somewhere behind the stage a voice said, "This is a story about a little boy named Peter." And all of us replied, "Oooooooh."

A little figure about as long as my two hands put together walked onto the stage all by himself. But he wasn't really a boy. He looked like. . . well, like one of those stick figures we had been drawing in first grade. How could that be? How could a stick-Peter come to life? Then Peter's grandfather came onto the stage, a bird, a duck, a wolf. They all moved and each one had a different voice. I was so glad I was in the front row because I could figure out they'd been made out of pipe cleaners bent into the shape of arms, legs, wings, the duck's bill, the wolf's tail. But that didn't explain how they moved. That was a hard one. Gradually I began to notice strings going up from each of the figures. I noticed the strings got tighter and looser. Was somebody behind the stage pulling the strings? Could be.

But at the same time I was figuring out the mechanics, I was breathing through my mouth, the story was so engrossing. I worried when the pipe-cleaner wolf swallowed the pipe-cleaner duck. You could see the duck riding around inside the wolf's stomach. The duck didn't seem to mind much, but I didn't think it should stay there very long. Then came the scene when Peter let down a rope to catch the wolf's tail. The rope was a long pipe cleaner bent into a hook. Slowly it reached down from the top of the stage, quivering all the way, and slowly, slowly, while we all held our breath, it worked its way into the wolf's looped tail, carefully inched up again, and then jerked the wolf up into the air and shook it. The duck fell out of the wolf's stomach and waddled away. We all cheered and clapped.

The rest of the day was gray and dreary, even though, as I remember, the sun was shining brightly. For I babbled all the way home with my mother but wasn't able to find the words in my six-year-old vocabulary to tell her what I had learned: that Lee was taller than I and magical and Mr. Sorensen was bigger than all of us and magnetic, but those little pipe cleaners on the miniature stage were the hugest of all; that the light glistening on those stick arms and legs shone brighter than a hundred suns; that I had changed since yesterday and was headed in a direction that wasn't on any map. But maybe I didn't have to explain. She smiled all the way home.

Warren Kliewer is a dramatist and playwright who lives in Secaucus, New Jersey.

When Somalis
Think of Canada,
They Think
"Safe and Secure"
by Mohamud Siad Togane

Two years ago a delegation of Somalis led by
Ambassador Mohamud Holif called on Ed Broadbent,
then director of the International Centre for Human
Rights and Democratic Development in Montreal.
They were there to discuss the possibility of Canada
advising Somalia on how to get back on the road of
democratic culture, peace, law, order—and the difficult
custom of settling differences of opinion regarding gov-
ernance at the ballot box instead of on the battlefield.

During the course of the discussion, Mr. Broadbent
expressed amazement that Somalis still had confidence
in Canada, given how Canada "disgraced herself and
betrayed the Somali people in Belet Weyn . . . I really
don't understand why you would want to have anything to do with Canada given our recent shameful
record," he remarked.

Ambassador Holif responded: "What happened in
Belet Weyn was a tiny, unfortunate, and insignificant
tempest in that bush town, blown way out of propor-

tion. And when you examine dispassionately the over-all record of the Canada-Somalia relationship from the early 1950s to the recent brouhaha, you will under-stand that Belet Weyn was an exceptional aberration."

He is right.

What most Canadians don't realize is that when Somalis think of Canada, they think automatically of a safe and secure place to run to. They think of Canada as a land kinder than home. A land that has given a haven to literally thousands of them displaced by war and famine.

When Somalis think of Canada, they don't think of former defense minster Kim Campbell, her motley crew, and the event they managed to conceal for a sea-son from the Canadian people.

They think of Margaret Laurence, who put Somalis on the world literary map in such books as *The Prophet's Camel Bell*, the most perceptive, the most astute book ever written on that *fenomenale* (as Laurence styled it) called Somaliland by an expatriate. She forewarned Somalis (in vain) about the looming threat of clanism, the most insidious form of racism, which was about to engulf and destroy their nation. They think of Laurence's *A Tree for Poverty*, the first and most magisterial English translation of Somali ora-ture (that is, our oral literature), which celebrates the wit and wisdom of the Somali genius.

And they think of *Heart of a Stranger*, in which she draws the best and the fairest portrait of their national poet and hero, Sultan Sayyid Mohamed Abdullah Hassan, whom she dubs the Somali Louis Riel and whom the Brits dismissed and derided as the "Mad Mullah." She pays homage to his courage and cunning, which kept the British imperium frustrated, angry, and at bay for 20 years. He was armed with only "the poem and the spear" and with the slogan, "Our country and creed are not for sale!" She encapsulates his fantastical—his detractors would say fanatical—career thus: "He fought a good fight; he finished his course; he kept the faith."

When Somalis think of Canada, they don't think of Defense Minister Art Eggleton, they think of Jack Laurence, Margaret's ex-husband, old man of the *ballahs* (water reservoirs), which he dug in the Somali desert for grateful nomads and their thirsty camels.

When Somalis think of Canada, they don't think of that scapegrace, the Canadian Boozeborn Regiment, and their bloodlust for *nignogs,* they think of the sober, God-fearing, Mennonite missionaries from Canada who have run the best schools and hospitals in Somalia since the early 1950s. Almost any Somali you meet today in Canada who speaks English either went to one of the mission schools or was taught by someone who was educated at one.

When Somalis think of Canada, they don't think of Lieutenant-Colonel Carol Mathieu and Lieutenant-Colonel Paul Morneault and their lack of guts and grace in Belet Weyn; they particularly remember and think of Merlin Russel Grove, a Mennonite from Markham, Ontario, who sold what he owned and left home in 1960 for that far country in the Horn of Africa, to give meat to the poor and hungry, drink to the thirsty, clothe the naked, visit the sick, and help educate her future generation.

With fondness and gratitude—and *shame*—the memory and the sacrifice of Merlin abide with all Somalis who knew that intrepid, young Canadian who arrived among them 37 years ago this month, armed only with love and compassion for their poor benighted country.

With *shame* because on July 16, 1962, in Mogadishu, Merlin was murdered in his office by a crazy Somali who thought he was defending Islam from a Christian threat. Ironically, Merlin had been fostering peace between the Moslems and the Christians of Mogadishu, encouraged by a similar successful effort in the village of Mahaddey Weyn, where he is still fondly remembered by both Moslems and Christians.

When Somalis think of Canada, they don't think of former defense minister Doug Young and his cowardly machinations. They think of the love and the courage of Merlin's widow, Dorothy, who went back to Somalia some two decades later, after her three children had grown up, to work as a nurse and minister to the needs of abandoned Somali children. She returned to Mogadishu, the same city where she witnessed the murder of her husband and was badly mauled in the same unprovoked attack that robbed her of her husband.

That is what Somalis think of when they think of Canada.

About 10 days ago, in a discussion with the leaders of the Toronto Somali community, the so-called Somalia Affair came up, that event that has been exercising the conscience of Canada for a long time—to the bemusement of the Somali community.

This is how Mohamed Fara'ada Ga'amaade spinned it: "More than half a million Somalis were murdered in Somalia, most of them women, children, and elderly. Many were deliberately starved to death by war profiteers. Nobody knows their names. Their murderers are growing fat in Mogadishu squabbling over the carcass of Somalia. Not one of them will be brought to justice; there won't be any inquiry or investigation of these murders in the *Mondo Cane* of Somalia, where murder and mayhem are today as common as Hawiye, Idor, and Darod donkeys. In fact, the same dirty dozen, the same murderers styling themselves as 'the President of Somalia' or 'the future President of Somalia!' are right now attending yet another international conference in Nairobi. Go figure that one out.

"Four years ago—when the eyes of the UN, the U.S., and the whole world were on Somalia, when we got our 15 minutes of infamy by the grace and courtesy of the Mogadishu back-alley bully and brigand, Mad Aideed—one of the dirty dozen, General Gabyo, taunted the UN at a conference it sponsored in Addis Ababa by challenging it, by throwing down the gauntlet, by saying to the UN: 'If you are really serious about solving Somalia's problems, arrest Aideed, arrest us dirty dozen right now. You won't get another golden opportunity . . . You really want to restore hope and sanity in Somalia, don't let us go back to Somalia. We are Somalia's heartache and headache. As the gypsies to whom we are related say: One madman makes many madmen and many madmen make madness.

"'We are the ones who are driving Somalia mad by dividing it into fiefdoms, insane asylums, clanships, cults, and countless clans. Arrest Aideed, our commander-in-chief-in-madness . . . We dirty dozen are all bald, as bald as the palms of your hands, and yet we are fighting to the death, we are murdering Somalia, over a comb. We want to be President of Somalia but there is

no Somalia; Somalia is dead; we dirty dozen killed it.
Arrest us for the murder of a nation, if you are really
serious! Or shall we just engage in *devillomatic* skul-
duggery and chitchat?'

"Everybody laughed. They thought it was a big
funny joke. If it were just a joke, no truer words have
ever been said in jest. Imagine the UN arresting anyone! Maybe that was the joke. Remembering how the
UN fueled the civil war in Somalia and enriched gangsters such as Mohammed Farrah Aideed, I can't help
but think of what Lyndon Johnson said of the UN
when Martin Luther King advised him to let the UN
settle the Vietnam issue: 'The UN cannot pour piss out
of the boot with the instructions written on its heel!'

"Thanks to Canada, the whole world knows the
name of Shidane Arone, but nobody knows the names
of the countless hundreds of thousands of Somalis murdered by the dirty dozen: That is the difference
between civilization and savagery; that is the difference
between decent Canadian people and the UN bureau-
crats who sit in glass houses pretending to throw
stones."

Everyone agreed with Ga'amaade, which surprised
him and everybody else: Unanimity is a rare jewel
among Somalis, briefly glimpsed and only heard when
they are at prayer in mosques chorusing, *"Ameen!"* to
Allah.

During our discussion the other day, Dalmar
Mohamud, a nephew of Ga'amaade, who is called the
real Canadian because he speaks only English and
French and not Somali, who is aptly named Dalmar,
meaning one who has travelled far across many lands,
for he was conceived in Mogadishu and was born 24

years ago in a Women's College hospital in Toronto, quietly concluded thus: "The so-called Somalia Affair is really about how Canada lost its virginity, its innocence, its international image as a nation of Good Samaritans and do-gooders.

"Many Canadians are hopping mad and are screaming 'Cover-up!'" I understand, it is sad and maddening. The ghost of Shidane Arone has not been laid to rest. It walks abroad in Canada haunting the soul of our nation. The only way we can exorcise it is to expose everything to the light. Accountability, not impunity! Let the chips fall where they may. This is no banana republic where the military dictate! The Canadian public shouldn't let the politicians and the top brass get away with the cover-up.

As Somalis say, "What is hidden stinks!" The cover-up stinks. Something is rotten in the state of Canada!

Mohamud Siad Togane is a poet who lives in Montreal and is a coordinator of ERGADA, a Somali peace organization.

Wardrobes:
Some Shopping Discoveries
by Janet Toews Berg

It was the year I turned 40 that I made the New Year's resolution to give up shopping. I am not ordinarily given to rash declarations, but something my husband said a few weeks before made me hit a mental Pause and Rewind. I had come from a shopping trip with a hot pink, cowl-neck, acrylic sweater and announced that I thought my wardrobe was now complete. My husband's response was, "I've heard that before."

Bringing home a hot pink item of any kind, I had to be prepared for remarks like, "Don't tell me, let me guess. It was on sale." Or "Hot Pink, dear?" The truth is neither my husband nor I are hot pink people; this purchase was a totally impulsive buy, based on a salesperson's comment that I looked good in pink. I was not prepared for, "I've heard that before." On the spot, I decided to live with a complete wardrobe for a year.

This resolution was not as impetuous as it may sound. It was consistent with a decision my husband and I made about five years before, when we went back to our roots and joined the Seattle Mennonite Church. As we became better acquainted with our highly educated, highly principled, urban Mennonite counterparts, we were captivated by their values of simple living and global awareness. In the process, our entire lifestyle and our we-deserve-it-because-we-spent-years-going-to-school-to-get-where-we-are attitudes were called into question.

Simple living was not a new concept to me, growing up in a family of nine children in rural Montana, but it was one learned from necessity, not choice. Now as an urban professional Mennonite with money and a "need" for professional clothing, I found that simple living was not so simple to achieve.

Prior to this fortieth year resolution, I made what I thought were some fairly dramatic simplicity statements when I gave up short skirts and high heels. Other fashion concepts and limitations followed: only natural colors, only natural fibers; then, washable fabrics. There was the consignment store phase, the only-small-shop phase, the only-Northwest-made phase, and the only-international-market phase. My search for simplicity in wardrobe acquisition had included just about everything except total abstinence.

During my resolution year I was able to see more clearly the deceptions that had kept me buying clothes: This piece is of lasting value. Buying this will save you money. You ought to buy this because you deserve it.

Every time I put on my wool gabardine, olive brown suit that year I was reminded of the Lasting Value line. I had bought the suit several years before, and it truly was a great basic outfit. "You will wear it for years, and you can wear it almost year-round in Seattle," were the words of the salesperson.

I was only going to buy the jacket at first, because it

went perfectly with the olive and maroon wool challis skirt I found for a bargain at a consignment shop. But the salesperson convinced me that I would be sorry if I did not buy the matching straight skirt. "You have three great outfits if you wear each with something else, and then the two together," she reasoned.

What she failed to mention is that the inherent nature of a basic outfit is to look downright dull unless one puts some accessory with it, something not basic, something colorful or frivolous. Every time I put on the suit, I couldn't just wear the jacket. One should wear things equally, shouldn't one, like rotating tires on a car? I felt the urge to go out and buy something to go with it. Yes, I could wear it for years, but at the price of new accessories every year.

All summer I pondered the Buy-to-Save-Money ploy used when I bought my natural linen, oversized jacket at the End-of-Summer sale several years before. Rarely had I been drawn to something as immediately as I was to this jacket. It was made by a Northwest designer; it was elegant and unlike anything else I owned. And it was on sale, nearly half off. The message given to me by the salesperson was the opposite of the Buying-Basics-concept. "This is such a unique and wonderful jacket, and you have saved so much money that you can go out and buy a basic dress or skirt to match and still save money."

But when does the statute of limitations end on money saved at a sale? With this particular item I extracted years of justification for purchases. No one piece was quite right. The cotton flannel skirt was a bit too yellow, the linen dress was a bit too gray, and the khaki silk skirt was too lightweight. All on sale, and all sales final. Sorry. Where was all the money I saved?

My fabulous Navajo-style outfit was neither basic nor on sale. It was full-priced, purchased with the You-Deserve-It coupon. The skirt was pieced together so that it had almost horizontal stripes, in a V-shaped, Navajo rug pattern—in navy, tan, and orange. The top was a navy, oversized blouse with a V-shaped inset in the back.

I didn't buy it for the reason that it was beautiful; in fact, I didn't buy it the first time I tried it on. I bought it because of the words of the shop owner, words that made me feel my name was written on the outfit: "You're so lucky you are tall. Most women would not even dare to wear this; look at the horizontal stripes. But it looks great on you." Not only was I lucky to be tall, the saleswoman told me, but implied that I was lucky to have found her. The fact that I was tall was the good news. Did I realize, though, that I had a high waist and sloping shoulders? Not to worry, though, because this outfit covered these problems beautifully.

Of course, there was the little matter of some accessories to go with it: soft, pliable shoulder pads— "Don't you just hate the pads that come with these clothes?"— and a wide Southwestern-looking belt with a big brass buckle. The message was: "You have defects that you have suffered for years [how did she know about those painful adolescent years when I thought I was a giant], but with these clothes you will suffer no more. You deserve to look good." At least she didn't tell me I would wear it for years. Now, a year later, the blouse looked like washed denim, and the skirt was too short.

After a few months, my once magical wardrobe took on the more realistic look of what it was: an accumulation of clothes—basics without accessories and accessories without basics, skirts too short or not the right hue or weight. With my new resolution, buying new clothes was not a choice, so I gradually diminished my obsession about what to wear to social events and began looking forward to conversations with people. I stopped looking in mirrors and took up inward reflection. I had more time for reading books and newspapers—about international affairs and about people who had more serious concerns than clothes. I came to know a world of people who had no care about how long skirts should be or how high the waist.

From somewhere in my scripture-memorization past came the verse from Romans: "Do not be conformed to this world, but be transformed by the renewing of your minds . . ." Transformation and renewal came not in finding an answer to the wardrobe dilemma, but in giving up the pursuit. The idea that one can find a unifying clothing principle was itself a delusion, a fantasy perpetuated by the fashion industry. Only when I stopped shopping could I begin to renew my mind instead of my wardrobe.

Being free of the quest for a complete, well-coordinated wardrobe allows me to buy clothes I like or nothing at all. Because my mind is being renewed, I need not spend time ruminating on the latest commercial temptation I seem prone to, or on how that single order from Lands' End could have resulted in the landslide of catalogs that came last Christmas, or on whether I should have ordered that 100% cotton cranberry turtleneck dress. I refuse to be undone by the fact that the dress was on sale, one-third off. It is a wonderful dress; I have worn it frequently, and its care has been easy as advertised. But why did I order the suggested belt (belt sold separately)? I already have this wonderful wide Southwest-looking belt with a brass buckle.

Janet Toews Berg is a psychiatrist and writer in Seattle, Washington.

Worshiping
with the Early Anabaptists
by John Oyer and Keith Graber Miller

No one knows much about early Anabaptist worship. Because we have few primary sources, the actual,
routine worship of our spiritual forebears remains
somewhat of a mystery. What we do know, however,
reveals a people committed to gathering for worship
though their lives were in danger, who wrote hymns
based on Scripture and experience, who prayed with
fervor, and who placed emphasis on both sermons and
sermon response from the congregation.

Testimony at court trials of Anabaptists and routine
reports of state church visitors throughout the 16th
century open small windows onto the worship practices of rank-and-file Anabaptists. One finds at most
bits and pieces of information, only rarely a description
of an entire worship service. The latter come primarily
from the Anabaptists' enemies: those who sneaked into
Anabaptist worship settings undetected to spy on these
illegal gatherings and report them to state authorities.

One of the most thorough reports was in 1576 from
Elias Schad, a Lutheran vicar at Old St. Peters in
Strasbourg and a teacher of Hebrew. Schad was committed to eliminating "sectarians" from Strasbourg territories. He and his co-workers were so successful that
by the end of the century, one account says that "no
sectarians remained in Strasbourg."

In his 1576 report of Anabaptist worship, Schad writes, "When I learned from trustworthy people that Anabaptists from many places were coming here under the pretext of attending the Strasbourg Fair and were going to have a meeting in a forest, as often happened, on St. Ulrich's night [July 4], I and several others, 13 in all, dressed in wanderers' clothing and left the town when the gates were about to be closed for the night. One by one we followed some Anabaptists and came upon two women, who, assuming us to be visiting brothers, helped us find the paths and by-ways as well as with their watchwords helped us to pass their guards posted at the entrance of the Eckbolsheim Forest."

Schad writes that people gathered in small clusters while leaders moved from group to group, perhaps checking whether all present were sympathizers. Once that was concluded, the group moved deeper into the forest.

One can't expect an extremely accurate account from a person seeking to eradicate those being observed; that's one of the fears about the few records we have about Anabaptist worship. We also must understand that Anabaptists were springing up in various parts of Europe in the 16th century, and not all strains developed the same forms of worship. Our findings here are based primarily on several published and unpublished archival sources covering the Alsace, the Duchy of Württemberg, the imperial cities of Esslingen and Augsburg, several principalities in central Germany, and Switzerland.

The Anabaptists continued to gather for worship, in spite of threats against their lives. For many decades in the 16th century and into the early 17th century, they were persecuted by sister Protestant and Catholic believers. While their movement included thousands of adherents throughout the 16th century, estimates are that in about 100 years, some 2,000 Anabaptists were killed at the hands of Catholic and Protestant governments.

To avoid persecution, the Anabaptists worshiped in forests, as in the Schad account, or in caves, barns, or mills—wherever they could find a hidden place. Only one Anabaptist meetinghouse was built in the 16th century, and that was in West Prussia in 1590. A few groups bought and refurbished the interiors of buildings like warehouses, but they were forbidden to make the exteriors look like conventional churches—even into the 19th century in some areas. We shouldn't be surprised about the Anabaptists not having symbols or sculptures or stained glass windows in their meetinghouses. Most of them didn't even have meetinghouses, and they got used to the simplicity of natural surroundings.

The Anabaptists circulated notes among themselves about when and where their secret worship meetings would take place. They, like the slaves in colonial America in later centuries, worshiped in fear. They worshiped nonetheless, because such corporate religious practices gave them the collective social and spiritual energy they needed to survive.

When Anabaptists worshiped in larger groups, the central element was preaching to explain the Scripture. The services included prayers and hymns, and participants also had the opportunity to comment on the sermon. Then they ate a light meal together, sometimes baptized candidates, and discussed major issues such as who among the ministers or readers would be the presiding elder. Smaller, more frequent meetings, with possibly five to 10 people present, included Scripture readings, interpretation, and prayer, but perhaps less singing than at larger, more secluded gatherings.

Although some Anabaptists purportedly wished to exclude singing entirely from worship services, there is evidence of singing from Anabaptism's earliest days. This wasn't the four-part harmony that many Mennonite groups are now known for, but there was singing. At a public execution in 1527, the Anabaptists sang, in Latin, Luther's hymn *"Veni, Creator, Spiritus"* (Come, Creator Spirit).

In 1535 a number of Anabaptists were arrested while worshiping in an old mill, 500 yards outside of a village in what is now east Germany. They were caught because townsfolk heard them singing hymns, one of them being the German hymn *"Komm, Heilige Geist"* (Come, Holy Spirit). Singing was a dangerous act, because it drew attention to the worshipers; for that reason it was avoided in some settings.

Anabaptists also were a part of the tremendous burst of hymn-writing energy of the 16th century. About 6,000 new hymns were written in this first century of the Reformation by Catholics, Protestants, and Anabaptists, a symbol of the explosive religious vitality of the era. The Reformed were singing the Psalms, and the Lutherans wrote full-blown hymns. The first Anabaptist Dutch hymnal was published in 1562, and the nucleus of the *Ausbund,* which the Amish still use today, was published in 1564. Scholars have been able to identify at least 130 Anabaptist hymnwriters.

The Anabaptists put to verse various accounts of

martyrdom, Scripture, and other material, much of it of a moralizing nature. The Anabaptist hymns included very little praise to God. Today the Amish continue the tradition of singing number 131 in the *Ausbund* at every service. It begins with a short praise to God for the goodness God has shown so graciously in bringing the worshipers together to admonish them.

Forms of prayer are even more difficult to identify in the scanty Anabaptist sources, even though *Martyrs Mirror* includes a number of prayers. The recent *Praying with the Anabaptists* (Faith & Life Press, 1994) likewise highlights particular prayers of our ancestors.

Elias Schad, in his 1576 account of the Anabaptist worship service he secretly attended, claimed that after the Eckbolsheim Forest sermons, Brother Peter [Walter] asked the gathered believers to pray. He writes: "Thereupon they scattered, all knelt, each usually before an oak tree as if he were worshiping it. The prayer lasted at least a good fifteen minutes, perhaps closer to thirty. There was a great audible murmuring as if a nest of hornets were swarming; they waved their arms and beat their breasts almost like priests when they read the mass . . . . They never raised their heads and they sighed and groaned and moaned like a tired old horse pulling a cart or wagon."

The melodrama is doubtful, but a 1545 account of another all-night worship service in the same forest mentions a prayer time that begins with moaning, sighing, and no words at first. That description says the group held special prayers for those in the fellowship and in other regions of the Anabaptist world.

There is evidence that the Anabaptists prayed the Lord's Prayer, although much of their praying was apparently extemporaneous. They didn't use prayer books in the early decades of Anabaptism, and much of their prayer was silent.

Anabaptist preaching, just as that of other 16th-century reforming groups, became the center of the worship service (in contrast to the eucharist in mass). According to Elias Schad's account, Brother Peter opened the meeting, producing "his soiled New Testament in the Swiss translation [Froschauer] and read a passage from the epistle." Then, the account continues, "The others did likewise, and although they all put on spectacles [they] still could not read well in that feeble light, [and] it was a laborious and not very edifying process. The Sermons, each of which lasted about fifteen minutes, seemed to me to have as much power as if chopped straw had been sprinkled over them."

Nearly every early Anabaptist sermon included something about repenting of one's sins and the grace of God in Jesus to forgive. Schad says the sermons he heard were about the Fall, about how our forebears had eaten sour grapes and set their children's teeth on edge, and about the suffering of Christ who redeemed them. "They emphasized especially that they should thank God for choosing them out of the world, for they were not in the world." (Here Schad adds his own humor: "They were truly not in the world but in the forest.")

Schad also notes that during the preaching, some stood, some leaned against trees, some were seated, some were lying face down, some were napping, and some were even in a deep sleep. Someone was appointed to walk through the crowd to shake them and say, "Get up, brother," or "Wake up, brother," or "Hear the word of the Lord!" At such worship services, the initial sermon sometimes lasted three hours, with the second (and sometimes third) sermons being much shorter. Because it was the middle of the night, and because attenders weren't able to get back into town until after the gate reopened at 6 a.m., it was expected that some would sleep during the service.

There is evidence that by the second half of the 16th century, when Anabaptists were sill a young movement, they were using the Gospels far more than the Epistles or the Old Testament, quoting them more regularly. They did use the Old Testament when preaching about salvation history, as the Old Order Amish do now. From the Gospels, the Anabaptists were most likely to choose Matthew, then Luke, and maybe some chapters from John; they rarely used Mark. This scriptural usage was true at least for the Swiss and South German Anabaptists but perhaps not as true for the Dutch, who were more acculturated and went more with the trend of the Reformed church.

The preaching tended to be admonition style. In court records, when Anabaptists were asked why they joined the movement, they said they'd heard someone preaching. When asked what they had heard being preached, they often noted that they had heard about sin and repentance. Sin, repentance, and an admonition to live a good Christian life were fundamental themes. Schad makes reference to Anabaptists' pharisaic piety, the notion that they were the best of all Christians. It is true that in the early years they may have said this about themselves. However, between 1550 and 1750, they were cited by others as the best of all Christians, though they themselves said little to nothing on the point.

Anabaptists were known to live moral, upright lives,

and they developed a reputation for being people of integrity and clean living. Early Anabaptist sermons often included stories about the results of being good to inspire others also to be like Jesus. This was partly because not all participants in worship were yet committed members. This was not just "preaching to the choir." It also was quite effective in the 16th-century context. The humanist and Greek scholar Erasmus had accused the Catholics and Protestants, somewhat unfairly, of not being moral. There was a large middle ground of people, whose intellectual leader was Erasmus, who were attracted to this moral preaching.

What is most distinctive about Anabaptist worship (distinctive from surrounding Catholic or Protestant groups) is related to preaching.

Among the Anabaptists a democratization began to happen in the preaching moment. As the Schad account makes clear, after the several sermons, others present were encouraged to speak.

Schad says Brother Peter called out in a loud voice: "Now, dear brothers, you have heard and understood the Word of God and have prayed earnestly. If there is anyone among you who has not quite understood, he should come here and we will instruct him! Or, if the Spirit of God reveals anything to someone to edify the brethren, let him come here and we will hear him in a friendly manner."

The innovation evident in this worship practice is that others in the congregation were encouraged to speak, not just the minister or the town-appointed preachers. Believers in the pews had a right to be heard. Such a democratization was based partly on 1 Corinthians 14:29-31: "Two or three prophets should speak, and the others should weigh carefully what is said. And if a revelation comes to someone who is sitting down, the first speaker should stop. For you can all prophesy in turn so that everyone may be instructed and encouraged."

The early Anabaptists used this passage to justify interrupting a Reformed preacher in the midst of his sermon or at its end. It is possible that for the Anabaptists sharing preaching or instruction in this way was a necessity, since many of the educated leaders were killed off quite early in the life of the movement.

In 1562, 21 Anabaptists were arrested after they were caught worshiping in a ravine. In the court record they are repeatedly asked who their leader is. "Well," they say, "our last leader died three years ago, in 1559." Then they begin to explain that Brother John sometimes reads a passage of Scripture, and Hans sometimes provides an interpretation, but so do Christian and George, and sometimes Felix reads the Scripture, too. Because leaders were particularly vulnerable, it may be that those arrested were simply protecting them; it's safe to assume, however, that the Anabaptists did practice plural leadership.

Maybe they made a virtue out of a necessity—since there were few strong, literate leaders, everyone needed to help out. Whatever the cause, this preaching method can be considered an early Anabaptist distinctive. This became known as *zeugnis,* "witness," and such commentary was open to anyone, even those who had quite contrary words to speak.

In Schad's description, when the service leader opened the floor to others, the Lutheran minister ventured forth with his own sermon. Schad said: "Dear brother and sisters! Although I really did not come here to preach but to listen, I like to be where God's Word is being proclaimed. But because Brother Peter has given me the opportunity I will, in the name of God as he grants me grace, also present something to you that is in accord with God's Word and will be edifying."

Schad went on to speak about infant baptism and excommunication, and the crowd became suspicious of his words. But Schad said, "Brother Peter urged tranquillity and appealed to the Last Judgment for those who had left the true faith and those who were in error."

Then Brother Peter gave Schad and his companions a guide to lead them safely back through the forest. Perhaps, in all of this, there are lessons for us.

John Oyer is professor emeritus of history at Goshen (Indiana) College. Keith Graber Miller teaches Bible, religion, and philosophy at Goshen College.

When I Am Old,
I Want to Be an Elder,
Not a Senior
by Katie Funk Wiebe

I write as an insider. No more does the waitress ask if I qualify for a senior discount. She just looks at me. I have crossed the border, but I don't know exactly when I did. I wrote about growing older when I was looking ahead to it. Now I know about aging firsthand. Some of my thinking has changed.

Personal experience of aging in a particular culture deeply shapes the way a person ages and what meaning it has for her or him. Within our society lies a deep dread and loathing of old age. It rubs off easily on those approaching this border. I've watched countless men and women do a soft-shoe dance for several years, sometimes for decades, at the threshold. "Am I old yet or am I not old?" these people ask themselves. "When do I know I am old?"

Maybe they can keep old age at bay if they keep up the appearance of youthfulness and don't associate closely with their age group. People who see "old" as a four-letter word fight the cycle of life. They avoid identification with their years the way some people avoid tofu. Successful aging, in their thinking, is to keep middle age going into their sixties and seventies.

One elderly woman once advised me, "Don't worry about getting old. You'll get older whether you worry or not." Somehow it happens: "Now I am old."

My greatest concern is not whether I can slow time by hanging onto a youthful face and form, but whether I can keep growing inwardly. Advertisers urge me to apply creams to my face to avoid wrinkles. I am more concerned about what to apply to my soul to prevent it from becoming a shriveled sack of bitterness, regrets, criticism, and irritability.

I see this stage of life as a time of grace. Old age is God's invention for completing the life cycle and preparing me for the step into eternity. I want to be able to praise God for this time of life. I want to experience the Gospel as good news to the end of life.

How is my inner life different now than it was 20 years ago when I was in my prime? Then I didn't have to pit culture's views of my age against my own feelings about myself as I do now. Then I was still forging ahead as far as career and reputation were concerned. Then I was in daily contact with people. Then something was expected of me daily.

Now I am one of a vast group of amateurs at aging who are trying to figure out what aging is all about in a more positive way than what our culture informs us. At the turn of the century, life expectancy was below 50 years of age. At the turn of this next century, it will be in the early eighties for woman and late seventies for men. My generation and those to come have been given an unexpected gift of years because of better nutrition, advanced medical technologies, and extended nursing-home care. So if aging is grace, it is also a challenge.

When I Am Old, I Want to Be an Elder, Not a Senior

I consider the way my mother aged. She never worked outside the home but moved through the life stages always very much engaged in the one same task: homemaking. Her identity never changed. Her relationships remained fairly stable. Yet I sense she worked at her aging. She remained alive and alert until her death at nearly age 99.

Somehow through the later years my mother picked up the identity of "elder" in her congregation. Not in the organizational structure, but in a spiritual sense. Everyone in her small congregation knew and respected Grandma Funk, one of very few old women in their small congregation. Yet she experienced increasing personal diminishment and disengagement from life. Aspects of aging troubled her.

Elderhood, according to Zalman Schachter-Shalomi and Roland S. Miller in *From Age-ing to Sage-ing,* is a state of consciousness that calls us "to engage in life completion, a process that involves specific tasks, such as coming to terms with our mortality, healing our relationships, enjoying our achievements, and leaving a legacy for the future." Taking on an identity as an elder is "an ongoing transformative process" enabling us to "harvest our lives, to bless all that we have lived through, and to convert this rich experience into wisdom."

The authors write that elderhood enables older men and women to become "spiritually radiant, physically vital, and socially responsible elders of the tribe." I want to be an elder when I am older.

I don't want to be a golden-ager, a euphemism used to take the harsh edge off aging.

I don't want to be a senior citizen. In the business and professional worlds, the word "senior" is a term denoting power, as in senior pastor, senior vice-president. That is not true for older adults. When "senior" is applied to them, it is a term meaning you can get a discount at business establishments.

I don't want to be a retiree because to retire means you have left something behind. A retiree is not a teacher or a businessman. A retiree is someone who has passed into a state of being who he or she is not.

I see that to become an elder is a big task, mostly a spiritual task. Yet my eldership and the eldership of today's baby boomer women will differ from that of my mother's.

Boomer women will face the same kind of identity crisis on retirement as men leaving a profession. Yet these same women have some decided advantages over men as they think of growing older.

They are more likely to be independent and self-sufficient, both financially and psychologically, than their mothers were. (Poverty, however, will remain a challenge to many single older women.) They enjoy better decision-making skills. Unlike many men, they have practiced withdrawal and reentry into the work world all their lives. They have had to make many adjustments during their lifetimes and will therefore not be as ready as my mother was to accept the aging blueprint society hands them. They will have spent more time in a greater variety of overlapping family roles than any generation in history—as child, spouse, parent, grandparent, stepparent.

Boomer women are more likely to have learned the skill of caregiving than men, having throughout a lifetime looked after children, parents, and even husbands. Some wives constantly monitor husband's bodies; they carry the pills, watch diets, and so forth. They worry more about possible widowhood than their own health.

Yet, despite the differences between the ways men and women approach the latter years, the spiritual task for both is to become an elder. The first part of the task, according to Schachter-Shalomi and Miller is *life completion.* I see this as acknowledging that death is not God's goof. It is not to be feared but to be accepted. My mother in the last weeks of life when asked by a nurse where she wanted to go when she was released from the hospital said openly, "I want to go to be with the Lord." The puzzled nurse didn't know what she meant. But Mother knew she was ready to leave this life.

A second spiritual task older adults face is *healing relationships through forgiveness.* Some of us may have a special assignment in this regard. In February 1997 I had a speaking engagement in Saskatoon, the place where many of my formative experiences of young adulthood took place. I found myself doing some intense soul-searching before going back to my old stomping grounds. Did I have anything to say to these people?

I often speak publicly about the need to release others through forgiveness to get out from under the load of unfair pain. One evening the Spirit told me it was time to forgive the Saskatoon Mennonite Brethren church council who, in 1946, after I had been elected leader of the youth group asked me to resign. Something about the shape of my body made the task impossible.

"Forgive," urged the Spirit.

"But this story is a great way to poke fun at the paternalistic church system," I responded.

"Forgive," said the Spirit. "What is on their conscience is their problem. Your task is to forgive." I forgave.

But that wasn't enough.

"Forgive the Canadian Mennonite Brethren Youth Committee who refused to allow you to become editor of *The Youth Worker* because you were a woman, even though you had been doing the work under your husband's name." I took care of that.

But even that didn't satisfy the Spirit. "What about the Sunday school superintendent who denied your request to teach a women's Sunday school class in Kitchener because women were not to teach in the church?" Would this list never end?

The spiritual task of some of us who carried the first painful brunt of opposition and often trivialization of women's ministry is to forgive and not carry those burdens into the afternoon of life. For other women, other grudges and hurts may have stockpiled in their memories. Aging is a time to forgive and let go.

Another spiritual task is *simplification*. It means in essence at some point saying, "Enough is enough. Enough doo-dads. Enough remodeling and buying new. Enough shopping. Enough adding to what you put on shelves and store in closets." My mother taught me well here. As her life became more circumscribed, she indulged in a frenzy of getting rid of things that occupy space. No garage sales for her. Just give it away. She knew no moving van would accompany her coffin to the cemetery. Today's boomer women who never knew the Great Depression may have a harder time letting go of things because they have been hounded by consumerism all their lives.

When I Am Old, I Want to Be an Elder, Not a Senior

Harvesting one's life, according to Schachter-Shalomi and Miller, is necessary for good living in old age. Real elders gravitate toward this task. Basically it means seeding the future with wisdom by sharing some of life's transforming moments. There is great power in storytelling. A civilization can be killed in a few generations if no one passes on the wisdom, not the information, of the elders.

I see this task as passing on my life smarts. Why hang onto my life after I have lived it? I do this through writing. Others do this through relationships with children, especially grandchildren, or mentoring younger women.

The all-encompassing task of elders then becomes *the need to craft one's life,* not just learn new crafts. The twin dangers of aging are isolation (because of widowhood) and self-pity, both of which lead to loneliness. Women and men bored and weary with life become boring and wearisome people—a species the other members of the human race soon avoid. Crafting one's life means remaining an interesting person because you are interested in others and in the shape your life is taking. That includes developing a relationship with God and learning to love the silence of solitude.

In 1988 I wrote *Bless Me Too, My Father.* I was asking for a blessing from the church upon my life as a woman in her early sixties. I knew what I wanted and needed.

What blessing should a 72-year-old woman ask of God? What about at 82? Or 92? Older women are in danger of thinking they have no future, they do not need to dream. A look at the lives of some of them, especially those in nursing homes, limited to half a room, a few personal belongings, seems too stark, too empty. I fear becoming just another old woman.

What blessing do I want?

I want to see my aging as God's gift to me. I want to be an elder.

I want to age without stigma. I want to be able to stand tall as an elder because I am a child of God, made in God's image, worthy of respect from myself and others.

I want the courage to reformat my thinking about aging so that this stage becomes a time of vibrant elderhood in a culture that speaks about it in empty euphemisms. For that I need companions, old and young, who support me on this untraveled road.

Katie Funk Wiebe is an essayist and writer in Wichita, Kansas.

Strawberry Jam
by Freda Zehr

When I was growing up in a little Mennonite community in McAlisterville, Pennsylvania, in the heart of Juniata County, days of summer were filled with freezing, canning, jelly-making, and even drying corn. Peeling peaches, seeding cherries, picking and capping strawberries, and pulling weeds all seemed tedious and endless to me, but indeed necessary tasks.

Later after marrying, my husband and I moved to the city. In spite of that, I acquiesced to my culture and upbringing and made a feeble attempt to keep up with the Mennonite "Joneses." I drove to search for farms and orchards for my summer fare, but my heart was not in it. After our children were older, I took a full-time job to supplement the family income as well as add fulfillment to my life. I was glad for an excuse to finally say, without guilt, "I don't have time to can and freeze." Well not entirely without guilt!

I felt that our youngest, Andrea, who came seven years behind the rest, missed out on an important learning experience of our past culture. I carried this nagging feeling of guilt about her deprived upbringing throughout her high school and college days.

I first began to feel less guilt when she and her future husband requested a canner and canning jars as a wedding present.

But this weekend I was completely vindicated. Andrea came with her new husband to visit us for the first time since their marriage two months ago. They came proudly bearing gifts. I sat at the table tonight feeling totally guilt-free as we feasted on squash and cucumbers grown in their own garden and bread slathered with delicious strawberry jam made by them.

Even dessert had a touch of my past with homemade pie, made from fresh cherries which they had picked from a friend's tree. Sitting there tonight I decided that just maybe the canning-freezing-store-up-for-winter urge is an inherited gene and not a learned behavior!

Freda Zehr is a writer in Wilmington, Delaware.

Ana-Baptism
by Scott Holland

"We are water. We are swept away. Desire begins in wet-ness. (We are) born out of longing, wet, not dry. We can always return to our place of origin. Water. Water music. We are baptized by immersion, nothing less can replenish or restore our capacity to love. It is endless if we believe in water."

—Terry Tempest Williams

A few years ago I presented a paper on "how stories save us" at a literary theory conference in Utah. Some ex-Mormon writers at the conference introduced me to the work of Terry Tempest Williams. Williams grew up Mormon in the region of the Great Salt Lake. Aware of my ongoing quarrels with my sectarian, Anabaptist heritage, my new friends thought I would appreciate how the literate, theological imagination of Terry Williams refused to split nature and grace.

Sectarian religious traditions, whether Mormon, Mennonite, or Brethren, tend to sharply divide the sacred and the secular. It is therefore not surprising that they express little enthusiasm for the Feast of Epiphany. Epiphany, of course, celebrates the manifestation of God in Christ to the Magi from the East. Those pagan Wise Men followed neither the voices of the angels nor the paths of the Hebrew shepherds to Bethlehem. They were guided instead by the stars. With the strange scents of Babylon on their bodies, they entered the manger with exotic gifts for the Christ Child.

This year the Old Testament lectionary readings for the first Sunday after Epiphany were from the Genesis creation narrative: how *ruach*—the breath, or wind, or spirit of God—moved over the waters. The New Testament lessons were on baptism. This rich imagery from the lectionary of orthodox and liberal Christendom was too wonderful for me to resist in the composition of January sermons and meditations, even for my "Anabaptist" audience.

The Magi from Persia, like Persian mystics, sages, and poets who followed them, such as Rumi, understood that the breath of the divine touched the primordial elements of life: Earth, Water, Fire, Wind. Many Christian mystics through the ages have likewise understood well how the metaphors and rituals of creative religion return us to our elemental passions: the waters of baptism are wet with the longings and losses of life.

Normative Anabaptsim has resisted such a sacramental view of the universe and its liturgical performance, in favor of an emphasis on a separate, holy community funded by a word above, not upon, the waters. Baptism into a churchly community too often signals a separation from culture and even creation. Some Anabaptist thinkers have even explicitly stated that the baptized, disciplined community or peoplehood is the only sacramental reality. Not earth, water, fire, or wind. Not body, breath, bread, or wine. In short, God inhabits ethics, not earth. This is one reason why ethics and aesthetics and church and creation have been pried apart in modern Anabaptist denominations and theologies.

My work has attempted to "rescue the best in Anabaptism" by suggesting that the early Anabaptist protest movement provided a necessary and strategic hermeneutics of suspicion of an established sacramental system that domesticated the wildness of earth, water, fire, wind, and the transcendent, for narrow religious, political, and economic ends. At its best, Ana-baptism reminded the religious that God transcended the official and orthodox readings of church, culture, and creation. God is Other. The angel is a stranger and the stranger is an angel.

At its worst, Anabaptism split nature and grace, and therefore body and soul, Christ and culture. My work from the pulpit, lectern, and page has attempted to return to the wonder of sacramental universe through the reminder that God is revealed not only through the spiritual proclamation of the word but also in the carnal manifestation of the world. The word indeed became flesh, but the flesh also becomes word, again and again.

Because the story of creation returns us to infinite mystery beyond all finite morality, there can be no metanarrative or master-image to domesticate either the wildness of creation or the wonder of transcendence. We look for icons, not idols. In an "Anabaptist aesthetics," then, all elements and all elemental passions are at best icons or traces, not idols, of the divine.

There can be no official "Christian art," for the waters of baptism flow from the vast waters of all creation. Like all elements of this large life, those waters are *mysterium tremendum*—mysterious, fascinating, and terrifying. Before creation knew word, it was water. Before religion became "morality touched with emotion," it was emotion. Even the orthodox Fathers of the Church insisted, "Grace presupposes nature; it does not destroy it but completes it." (Thomas Aquinas)

We are saved by water and word, the Gospel teaches. As an Anabaptist preacher, I am reminded by the waters of baptism that aesthetics precedes ethics because the story of creation precedes the story of the church. Creativity is endless if we really believe in water.

Scott Holland is a pastor and writer in suburban Pittsburgh, Pennsylvania.

Erica

by Ed van Straten

Until a year ago we were used to seeing Erica come to church in her own adapted car. At the parking lot she would open the door, put out the parts of her wheelchair one by one, assembling them as she went, wriggle herself into the chair before she clicked the last part in place, lock the door of the car, and put her hands on the wheels of her chair, giving them a good push.

In earlier times Erica had been a promising sportswoman. But some minor surgery triggered a condition known as "post-traumatic dystrophy," meaning the muscles of her legs started to deteriorate. But every Sunday she showed us how strong her arms were, how deftly her fingers assembled—and after worship disassembled—her chair. Erica was, though a person with handicaps, an independent young woman. Educated both as a schoolteacher and a nurse, she had a job that was an ideal combination of the two: she was a teacher in a nurses' training school.

Erica was a leader in the children's program of our church, and sometimes she contributed to the beauty of the worship by playing flute, as a soloist or along with the organ. It was so normal to see her in our midst that we hardly noticed how she fought against the literally crippling facts in her life. But she did, for Erica did not believe in fate; she believed in faith. Some of us did see that.

Until a year ago. In the adapted house in a nearby town where she lived by herself (helped by friends), her custom-made bed suddenly collapsed. The builder had not secured it well enough. Erica, after some time, was found on the floor and rushed to the hospital. When I first visited her there about two weeks after the accident, all she could move were her eyes and lips. She could speak and swallow, though eating and drinking were not easy. Whatever else had been damaged in Erica, her fighting spirit had not been. The next time I came to her hospital bed she said, "Look! I can move my shoulder!" And indeed, she could move her shoulder, ever so slightly. You had to look very carefully to notice it, but, yes, Erica could move her shoulder.

Several months later Erica was taken to another hospital that specializes in putting people, so to say, back on their feet. The medical staff there did not think that Erica would ever walk again. They decided to help her in a different way. First, they told her she could not stay, if within two months she would be unable to feed herself. She cried when she told me that.

She still could only move her shoulder a bit and lift up her left hand—just a few centimeters. She could only move her head a few millimeters to the right and to the left. She could not sit up by herself. How would she ever manage to feed herself in two months' time? But she managed. Within two months she could bring a spoonful of food to her mouth—slowly, haltingly— without spilling all of it.

This hospital is not putting Erica back on her feet literally, but it does the next best thing: it trains her left arm and her left hand (she can't do anything with her right hand). And now she can move her arm a bit; she can wiggle her fingers.

Sometimes I ask her to press my fingers with hers. She tries, but has not yet the strength to really do so. But she can manage a sophisticated electrical wheelchair, and quite skillfully. As soon she was sure she could handle the chair by letting her fingers softly play on the buttons under her hand, she rented a wheelchair bus. My wife and I joined her for the ride and heard how she gave the driver the address of our church. Since that first time Erica is coming to church again. Not too often, for it is a rather expensive trip, but one of the members of our church is making it financially possible for her to come every once in a while. Of course, the church has also been coming to her, for many of us regularly visit her.

I remember the way people looked when Erica drove her wheelchair into the church that first time. It was as if suddenly the sun had come through on a bleak day. Probably not everybody realizes what it has cost Erica to come this far, but most of us do. Erica has become our sunshine, a living message about the meaning and the quality of life. There she is, part of our worshiping community and contributing strongly to it by "simply" being there.

Erica is working on another project: she wants to go home. After some deliberation the local authorities in her hometown agreed to provide money for further adaptations to her house—including a hoist she can handle herself that will lift her from her bed and put her down in the wheelchair, and the other way around.

She has already learned to do that. A young dog is being trained to help her—for example, to open or close doors. Nurses are ready to give her necessary support at home.

Erica thinks everything through—the type of telephone she needs, what she needs to heat water and make tea or coffee. She thinks about the best place for her bed in the bedroom so she can use the hoist optimally. And then she contacts the right people and asks them to do the things she needs. She organizes her life by using her brains, her voice, and by lifting a finger.

The last time I visited Erica she showed me a colored drawing. I thought it had been given to her, but, no—she had made it herself. It had taken her several months to make it with her weak, left-hand fingers. But she did not give up. She finished it. Of course. She has had hard times, sad days, moments when everything seemed to fall apart—but Erica does not believe in fate. She believes in faith.

Ed van Straten is a Mennonite church leader in EL Leidschendam, The Netherlands.

A Sermon

A Wedding Sermon
by Marcus Shantz

The first thing to say, Sheri and Mark, is that what you're doing is crazy. Today you're making rash, risky promises. Today you say to each other what Ruth said to Naomi: "Where you go, I will go, where you stay, I will stay. Your people will be my people, and your God my God. Where you die, I shall die, and there be buried. Nothing but death will part me from you."

Today you're becoming a new creature, a married couple. And we're all looking at you the way we look at newborn babies: we're amazed by your innocence and potential, by the mystery of what you'll grow to be.

It's crazy, getting married. Foolish. Daring. Bold. Not because of cautionary statistics that predict lame success rates for modern marriages. Not because of how enormous and overwhelming a lifelong commitment may seem. No, it's crazy for much older reasons. When you marry, you make a promise in the presence of God, and when you do that, anything can happen. It's crazy because of who God is.

In *The Lion, the Witch, and the Wardrobe,* Mr. Beaver tells Lucy that Aslan is wild. He's not a tame lion. "Who said anything about safe?" he says. "'Course he isn't safe. But he's good." Later on in the story, Aslan the Lion carries Lucy and her sister in a ride that is joyous, playful, breathtaking, and scary—all at the same time. And that's what you're in for—God carrying both of you to God-knows-where; the wind rushing past, the two of you both laughing and covering your eyes all at once.

People who make promises in the presence of God end up on unexpected adventures. This is surely one of the lessons from the Bible, which is full of characters who've made deals with God: Jesus, Moses, Mary, Abram and Sarah, Isaac and Rebecca, Jacob and Rachel. Joseph. And Ruth, whose words you've used to describe your commitment to each other.

Ruth was from Moab, which bordered on Israel; she was married to one of the sons of Naomi, an Israelite immigrant. Naomi's husband and two sons died, and Naomi, overcome with bitterness, prepared to return to her home, Israel. Her daughters-in-law, Ruth and Orpah, asked to go along with her. But Naomi dismissed them, and quite harshly at that: "Look," she said. "Go back to your people and your gods. I have no more sons for you to marry, and besides, Yahweh's against me. Get lost." Orpah left, but Ruth persisted, and responded to Naomi's despairing speech with those words that sound so much like a wedding vow. "Where you go, I will go. Your people will be my people. Your God will be my God."

Who knows why Ruth chose to go with Naomi? Probably it was part genuine kindness and part self-interest. There wasn't, after all, much left for her in Moab—an empty house full of old memories. Whatever the reason, Ruth stuck with Naomi, and that commitment took her to a strange land, to the town of Bethlehem.

They arrived together with no money, no home, and no livelihood. Naomi remained depressed and asked people to call her Mara, which means "bitterness." Ruth, meanwhile, decided to make the best of it and went out into the fields to gather the scraps of the barley harvest, picking up what the reapers left behind. She had good luck: she met Boaz, a wealthy farmer and relative of Naomi. Boaz, impressed by her care for her mother-in-law, made sure Ruth had more than enough grain. When Naomi discovered that Ruth had met Boaz, she regained some interest in life, and, to make a long story short, Naomi hatched a plot to marry Ruth to Boaz. It worked. Everyone lived happily ever after. At the end of the story Ruth has a son, Obed, who ends up being David's grandfather, so, according to biblical genealogy, Ruth is an ancestor of Jesus.

It's a marriage story. But oddly, it seems like the relationship between Ruth and Naomi—rather than Ruth and Boaz—is the more instructive for you today. Boaz, to be sure, seems like a good guy in the story and acts decently according to the marriage laws of his culture. But Ruth is the innovator, and her impulsive, voluntary promise to Naomi sets the tone and direction for the entire story.

I am not suggesting that we should pay special attention to how Sheri should relate to Brenda, or Mark to Sharon Lee—though these relationships must be important. I'm suggesting, Mark and Sheri, that you're both Ruth. And sometimes you'll take turns at being Naomi. And there are things you can learn from this story.

For starters, Ruth's promise to Naomi took her on a journey, and it was a journey to a place she probably would rather not have gone. A strange land with a strange language and a peculiar God. Israel, remember, was not much of a country by the standards of the day. Far from centers of power and money. Unglamorous boonies. A place you reached via backroads. The people—rustic at best, smelling of sheep and garlic. But it was also a promised land—a country where Ruth experienced God's grace and kindness in unexpected ways.

Don't be surprised, Mark and Sheri, if your marriage takes you down backroads. Perhaps literally, but also relationally, vocationally. Spiritually. That's where you'll find confidence and trust and love—on the soul's dirt roads. Navigating them together. I read this poem by Bronwen Wallace, and I thought of you:

> You'll take a map, of course, and keep it
> open in front of you on the dashboard,
> though it won't help. Oh, it'll give mileages,
> boundary lines, names, that sort of thing,
> but there are places yet
> where names are powerless
> and what you are entering
> is like the silence words get lost in
> after they've been spoken.
>
> It's the same with the highways.
> The terse, comforting numbers
> and the signs that anyone can read.
> They won't be any good to you now.
> And it's not that kind of confidence
> you're after anyway.
>
> What you're looking for are the narrower,
> unpaved roads that have become

the country they travel over, dreamlike
as the spare farms you catch
in the corner of your eye,
only to lose them
when you turn your head. The curves
that happen without warning
like a change of heart,
as if, after all these journeys,
the road were still feeling
its way through.

*　*　*

You, who have lived your whole life believing
if you made enough plans
you wouldn't need to be afraid,
driving through a countryside
only the road seems to care about,
to rediscover every time it enters
with that kind of love that's partly tenderness
and partly a sort of confidence
you can't put words around.

I know there's a pop song that assures us that "life is a highway." That the exits are clearly marked, that directions are easy, and that the course is clear. Both of you like having plans. Having maps. But it's not going to happen that way. Careers, education, where to live, kids . . . these will all pull you away from the five-year plan. Off of the highway and onto the backroads. There the signage isn't so clear; the directions are ambiguous. Don't worry about it. Talk it through together. Trust.

Naomi became bitter because she was surrounded by death. Her husband and sons—dead. Her aspirations for life in Moab—dead. Her speech to her daughters-in-law as she prepares to return home is the height of bitterness: "What are you waiting for—I don't have any more sons for you to marry." Ruth did more than ignore those words; she rejected them. Because she cared for Naomi, she challenged her with an alternative vision for their lives. "Where you go, I will go. Your people will be my people."

Ruth stood with Naomi in spite of her dismissiveness and despair. Even though she was surrounded by death. When they arrived in Bethlehem, Naomi's hometown, it was Ruth, the foreigner, who took the initiative while Naomi sat at home, depressed. Ruth supported and cared for Naomi even though Naomi claimed not to care much about anything. And sometimes that's what you'll need to do for each other. Because death is out there. There will be disappointments. Dissipated hopes. Failures. Things to be sad about. Those backroads aren't always easy.

When Ruth arrived in Bethlehem, she decided to go out into the fields and collect scraps. It seems to go that way for people who make promises with God. The complete package, the full meal, the final answer—rarely does God dish these things out. Instead, God provides scraps—fragments, clues, moments—things that may be useful if you're willing to be creative.

Scrap-collecting is a discipline of marriage, and there are a few good activities I can suggest that can help you with this skill.

The first is to listen to jazz every once in a while. Listen to how good jazz musicians improvise. As they play, they take fragments of melody and turn them into intricate, energetic music.

Mark, I remember a few years ago, you had me listen to a piece of music—a Bach violin duet, I think. You made me notice how the two violins intertwined in a complex and beautiful pattern, and you commented that it would be neat to play that at a wedding. A metaphor for marriage. Two voices, two lives, playing in perfect pitch, tempo, and harmony.

I like disagreeing with Mark, and I'd suggest that marriage isn't a duet but a trio. And it's more like jazz than Bach. Bach violinists know their music from beginning to end; jazz artists make it up as they go. Listen to Ella Fitzgerald sing live in Berlin. She's at her best when she forgets her lyrics and scats her way through. So you must learn to improvise when the words escape you.

And like Oscar Peterson or Holly Cole, you're making music with three players. Sheri, Mark, and a third musician. A third voice that occasionally leads out strongly. But more often than not it plays subtly, suggesting new directions in a still small way. Listen for it. You three must learn how to play together. You will each take cues from the other. Each will take turns at leading and at being led. You'll learn to trust each other's instincts, learn faith in the music you create together.

Second, take time to cook together. When you make food together, you nourish each other, and time spent preparing food is good and holy. Learn recipes, and then stray from them. Invite friends for dinner. Make soup and bread—it doesn't have to be elaborate. And use leftovers. In the *More With Less Cookbook*, there's a section called "Gather Up the Fragments." Read it; it's helpful. Old lasagna becomes soup. Old carrots become cakes. Old bagels become chips. It's miraculous what you can do.

Third, become quilters. At least become figurative quilters. Put a patchwork on your bed and notice the pattern formed from the scraps and swatches of material. Let the quilt become a reminder of all of your family and friends, of events and memories. You're good at this already. Take a look around you now and see the quilt you've made of us. We who are with you today are the scraps you've stitched together, and we're here to keep you warm. Remember that you can wrap us around you when you need to.

No, there's no telling what adventures God will lead the two of you into. He isn't safe, after all. He's not tame. But he's good. In the meantime, cook leftovers. Listen to jazz. Explore backroads, and trust that they eventually lead to the promised land. Gather the scraps and fragments that God provides. And each day of life, take up your threads and make yourselves a marvelous quilt.

Marcus Shantz writes and teaches in Kitchener-Waterloo, Ontario.

Humor

Home on the Range in Lancaster, Where One Buffalo Still Roams

by Sam S. Stoltzfus

Buffalo on the loose in eastern Lancaster County? Yes siree, 12 of them, 750-pound bison bulls. Roamed over Salisbury Township and beyond, and the Welsh Mountain foothills, they did, some for over eight weeks. One still at large. *Vas is los?* (What's up?)

Seems there was this Jake Stoltzfus (Little Jake in Amish circles) of Leacock Township, Amish cattleman, enterpriser. Practical Republican he is, Jake decided to try a new venture: Fatten buffalo bulls. Since the fat cattle market is as low as a sick steer's nose, Jake decided to try his hand at producing buffalo steak. And another reason: Jake had just purchased a nice farm along Plank Road in the White Horse hinterlands.

So the thought came: Run buffalo in the large meadow. The Pequea Creek flowed through—thus cheap buffalo grazing. With lots of Lancaster County sunshine and plenty of Pequea Creek water, said bison would soon be as docile as fat steers, so Jake thought. *Das war letz.* (That was wrong.)

Home on the Range in Lancaster,
Where One Buffalo Still Roams

So he purchased his 12 fat buffalo, which arrived at their Plank Road address in late April, and they just loved it, romping in the meadow, drinking from the creek, behaving like fenced-in bovines should.

Then, on that historical day, May 3, one of the buffalo found an escape route where the fence crossed the creek. Quickly, in buffalo lingo, he informed the rest of the clan, and they're off, tails in the air, snorting through the vast Pequea plains. *Dot geh'n sie.* (There they go.) Maybe hoping to get to their ancestors' birthplace 1,500 miles west.

And romp and roam they did, through Salisbury and West Caln townships, stampeding through young corn, lush alfalfa, ripping through fences as if through spiderwebs. They tore across tobacco patches, got into gardens, and splattered up front lawns. *Mach die frau base.* (Makes the wife mad.) And they got into pastures with Holstein heifers for buffalo blind dates.

No instructions in the township code book about how to catch buffalo. Not yet. But the word was out: If you see a shaggy buffalo, call Jake Stoltzfus pronto. Provided he hears his telephone ring, he'll call Sam Kinsinger, who will grab his trusty dart carbine, call his pickup-truck driver, Al Workman, and head off to Pequea Valley.

Not since Henry Lapp's 180-horsepower tractor ran off and dashed two miles cross-country—finally plowing into his neighbor's barn—was there such excitement in the *unter beckway* (lower Pequea), so we Amish call it. Sam and Al would drive to the buffalo area, carefully stalk the target buffalo from downwind to within 50 yards, take careful aim, and zing.

If hit, said buffalo would take off, and the chase was

on. Pickup truck and crew dashed after the beast through fields and lawns until the tranquilizer took effect. The beast turned turtle; the crew could truss him up, and four or five hefty men would throw the sleeping bison on the pickup bed and dash back to the Plank Road meadow. Quick—untie it before it comes to. *Noch ains g'fanga.* (Caught another one.)

Farmers plant their crops, spray for weeds, cultivate, and watch things grow, and they take a dim view of any man or beast that treads thereupon. So these buffalo ripping through fields were mighty unpopular. Henry Lapp (he of the tractor), another practical Republican, says, "If I see one, I'll shoot it with my 30/30 and it will roam no more."

In the old days, there were two Amish cowboys who had trained cow ponies and could rope them like Western cattlemen. Leroy Esh and his trusty steed, Queen, along with his hired man, Elam Zook and his mount, Maple, could rope heifers at a dead gallop.

Once, down in Nine Points, a farmer's 15 heifers went wild, roamed Bart and Colerain townships for two days. Leroy and Elam roped them all. Some Lancaster Stockyard professional horsemen who were called out gave up the first day. But today, Leroy and Elam, both gray-haired and their horses gone, don't take to roping any more.

So Jake and his buffalo-catching hands, Sam Kinsinger and Al Workman, had to do as they could for weeks. The buffalo crashed through the hinterlands, growing wilder and more feisty. One was shot three times, but into the woods he'd go. No one could find him. The beast got away again: *Kann mich net fanga.* (You can't catch me.)

Home on the Range in Lancaster,
Where One Buffalo Still Roams

Not since Revolutionary War soldiers roamed the Compass area and were fed in the Welsh Mountain foothills, during Washington's Valley Forge campaign, was there such a commotion in the *unter beckway.*

For 10 weeks, Jake and his crew chased these critters, catching them one by one. One was caught the first day, two the next day (Sunday), and finally all but one, which, as mentioned, is still considered to be at large.

So the word is out: Watch and look for the buffalo. Perhaps he is still indeed at large, or perhaps he's gift-wrapped and stacked in someone's freezer. The mystery of the lost Pequea buffalo. *Wu is er?* (Where is he?)

Sam S. Stoltzfus, formerly a farmer, now works in a machine shop near Gordonville, Pennsylvania.

Some Lists
by Craig Haas

Top Ten Reasons Mennonites
Lack a Tradition of Football

10. What good is a pigskin if you don't stuff it with sausage and potatoes?

9. Bad experiences with uniformed men invading our territory.

8. Players keep grabbing the coin before the toss is completed.

7. All the kneeling and standing is a little too liturgical.

6. We're still unclear about goals.

5. Too much touching on the backside.

4. We did away with the bench long ago.

3. Why stand around at halftime when there's work to do at home?

2. Chin straps make us look too much like Beachy Amish.

1. Not enough time in the huddle for everyone to "share."

Top Ten Ways
the Old Testament
Would Be Different
If Mennonites Wrote It

10. More genealogies.

9. Psalms arranged for four-part harmony.

8. Pot-luck Passover.

7. Still 12 tribes, but 20 separate churches.

6. Books of prophets end with martyr stories.

5. Sacrificial laws replaced by hearty recipes (provision made for "burnt offerings").

4. No more Song of Solomon.

3. Cities of refuge become suburbs.

2. Abraham doesn't plead for Sodom.

1. Pork is okay, but wine isn't.

Top Ten Four-Letter Words
Mennonites Love
by Craig Haas

10. SALE

9. FOOD

8. SING

7. MEET

6. SAVE

5. WORK

4. VOTE

3. FARM

2. CITY

1. FREE

Top Ten Four-Letter Words Mennonites Hate
by Craig Haas

10. HATE

9. BEER

8. ARMY

7. LOAN

6. FLAG

5. PAST

4. VOTE

3. OATH

2. SEXY

1. * * * *

You're Really a
Mennonite When . . .
by Craig Haas

. . . you believe every word of the Bible—including all those you've never read.

. . . at a church conference, you no longer feel like you're crashing someone else's family reunion.

. . . you want your church to be just like other churches, but to keep its separate identity.

. . . you think the Delmarva Peninsula sounds like it was named after a Mennonite.

. . . you can make a little go too far.

. . . you think of persecution, harassment, and martyrdom as the good old days.

Craig Haas is a philosophy professor and writer living in Mt. Joy, Pennsylvania.

A Murder Story

A short comic drama by Merle Good

[Narrator enters with a big book in hand. No set needed. Narrator speaks fairly rapidly.]

OK, hey, whatever. I don't want you laughing at my big book here. But I'll come to that—when I do my Bible verse about peace. I should say—right off the top—just to clarify—this is the actual murder weapon—it has a bit of blood on it—but we'll get to that.

I have to say—as sincerely as I can—that I'm for peace and all—I think I am—I mean, you never can be sure of your motives, can you—boy, this book's heavy!—*[shifts book to other hand]*—I mean, I think I'm for peace—like, why not—except some stuff is a little confusing to someone like me, I guess.

For instance—just take "struggle"—I mean, does that fall into the peaceful category?—you know, we learn in school about struggle—plant life, for instance—you know, green shoots pushing and struggling through the soil—that's very disruptive, if you think about it—and I've always been told that disruption and peace are not the same thing—although we're encouraged to struggle for peace, aren't we—and when you stop to think about it, some of these peace marches can be disruptive—so

I'm really not clear about the whole struggle mess and peace, for instance—but—

Take competition—can a peacemaking Christian, in good conscience—I know I'm talking purist here, and all—*[shifts book]*—can—or should—a Christian peace-and- justice type be against competition—at least in its raw form—like sports—I mean, competition means someone wins and someone loses—but isn't peace and justice about everyone winning—"No losers in heaven"—that type of stuff—I'm up, only when you're up—works for me!—whatever—

Now about this book—oh, yes, I wanted to say too that competition can affect everything—even grades—you know, tests—if I get the top grade, you can't—so wouldn't a Christian peacemaker type decide to sacrificially take the lower grade so others could go higher—as the Bible says, "Blessed is she who covets not the highest hill, but is at peace with the lower grade"—whatever—

And I know that brings up the whole passive/active thing which I admit I've never been able to fully understand and comprehend to the extent that some others seem to—at least they talk on and on about it—I mean, to me, "passive" is when you let something go by you—and "active" is when you let yourself go by it—so I've never really understood the cosmically dissected, super differentiated transpolarized realities—I mean—*[staccato]* it goes by me—or—I go by it—why get all peacefully stressed out—I mean, I could miss it.

Anyhow—this big book is called—(reading from cover of big book) **Strong's Exhaustive Concordance of the Bible**—you know what concordance means—**Words of Jesus in Red—and New Easy-to-Read Print—James**

Strong, S.T.D. and L.L.D.—*[polite smile]*—In any case, my dad was getting ready for some talk he had to give about peace or something, sitting at the table on the third floor of our house—we live in the city—when he thought he felt something on his leg—his pants, really. So he lifts his eyes from **Strong's Exhaustive Concordance of the Bible, Words of Jesus in Red** and sees that a small creature is making its way up his pant leg—almost to his knee, in fact—a mouse, actually—or, should I say, a creature of the mice family—whatever—this sucker seems to be in a stupor—half drunk or half drugged or something—just slowly creeping up my dad's pants, weary step after weary step—*[shifts book]*—

Now my dad's not a warrior, so to speak—I mean, I'm not saying he's not brave—but it did scare him, there on the third floor of our house on that dark night—and he reacted rather violently—he swatted this—mousal creature—to the floor in one swat—my dad's strong—but then he runs downstairs to my mom and tells her about the whole incident.

Now the mouse is still alive, upstairs, and my dad has to finish his talk—it's Saturday night—so what should he do? Unfortunately, I'm not home to help him out, and my mom's not the killer type. So he gets up his courage and goes back upstairs, sticks his head around the corner and sees this poor mouse standing in the middle of the floor, sort of swaying back and forth—like one of those fake dogs some people have on the rear ledge of their cars, inside the back window—and does my dad take pity? Oh, no, he gives in to his fear, really—and he runs and grabs **Strong's Exhaustive Concordance of the Bible, Words of Jesus in Red,** and flings it across the room *[throws book so that it lands with loud noise]*—

and—I'm ashamed to say—smashes (!) that poor, defenseless, possibly starving, possibly diseased mousal creature!!

[*Slowly and meaningfully*] I admit that I lost respect for my dad when I heard the story of the —"mousicide"— and it's raised a lot of questions for me—Is life fair?— Should my father have been more passive, more non-resistant?—Was there another way out of this tense situation?—Was the response proportionate to the threat?

[*Most sincerely*] Sometimes things like this make us grow up faster than we were meant to—it makes one really wonder—is there no place in the peaceable kingdom—for mice?

In any case, I seldom go to the third floor in our house anymore—I get squeamish walking by the scene of the crime [*walks over to slowly pick up the book, kicks imaginary dead mouse out of the way, wipes a bit of blood off the book, and continues*]. And I haven't really used **Strong's Concordance**, until trying to choose a verse to share with you this morning—did you know there's a page and a half of verses in here that use the word peace? —anyhow—I finally settled on a verse—one in red print, of course [*opens the book to read*]—

It goes like this—"My peace I give to you, not as the world gives." [*closes the book*] I haven't figured it out— but I like it—whatever. In any case, that's my murder story. Thanks.

Merle Good of Lancaster, Pennsylvania, is a writer, dramatist, publisher, and a co-editor of this volume.

Short Fiction, II

Souls of the Caribbean Sun
a short story
by Rafael Falcón

We had just backed up to turn around on a dead-end street when one of the back wheels got stuck in the steadily deepening snow. The search for an address in this university city we had just recently called home had brought us to the unfamiliar area. I kept pressing the accelerator, trying to liberate both our old vehicle and ourselves from this frozen entrapment on that cold, cold, January night. Yet the wheel continued digging a deepening hole, worsening our situation and soiling those famous white feathers, falling endlessly like the torrential rains of the tropical paradise I had left behind.

It was late and the situation was not improving. I was concerned about my wife, our three-year-old, but especially about our other son, a newly born infant. This secondary street did not seem to invite activity of any type, much less on a cold snowy night in the Midwest. Nobody seemed aware of our difficulty. No one, that is, except for one curious neighborhood resident. I had seen the movement of curtains opening in a nearby house and a man's face silhouetted against the pane, apparently checking on the action in his front yard. That was it. In my feeling of helplessness, a shadow of homesickness settled over me. If I were back home, a growing group of people would be gathering around us by now, curious but ready to help. Good-naturedly they would push this car out of its trap, like the helpful bystanders who years prior had liberated my parents' yellow '57 Chevy from its muddy dirt-road rut in *el campo* in Puerto Rico. All six of us children were there to appreciate that event.

In the absence of such assistance, I suggested to my wife that she handle the steering wheel while I would do some manual persuasion. After just a few minutes of such endeavor, my hands and feet felt several times more frigid than I had ever experienced in my whole life on the Antilles island. While I pushed on that heavy pile of vehicular metal, my mind traveled several thousand miles south. I began to think about the warmth and hospitality of my people, the gentle waves caressing palm-studded beaches, the fresh evening breezes rustling green banana leaves, and about a distant language whose idiosyncrasies I understood so well. Spanish, the voice in which I could express myself easily, transcended my current status of feeling like a child of limited speech ability, or feeling ignored because of my accent.

At that moment the slamming of a door abruptly interrupted my thoughts. I looked up to see a car parked a short distance away and two men approaching. The shorter one spoke first, "Do you need some help?"

I though I detected a recognizable accent very sweet to my ears and spirit, and I wanted to ask him if he was Hispanic. Yet in my short time on the university campus I had quickly learned that a person who looks like me may in fact speak another of Planet Earth's many languages. Caution curbed my enthusiasm and I responded in English with my nearly frozen tongue doing irreparable damage to pronunciation, "Yes, I do need help."

"*Pues, vamos a meterle mano,*" he said, looking at the taller one, who up to this point had remained quiet. "Let's get to it," he repeated as though suddenly aware he had spoken in Spanish.

My heart gave a leap of joy! "You speak Spanish?" I asked enthusiastically.

"Sure, *chico,* I come from the Dominican Republic and my friend is from Cuba."

"Well," I exclaimed, "looks as if we have here the Caribbean Alliance that many patriots and politicians have dreamed about. I am *boricua!*"

Not even the bright tropical sun that warms each of our respective islands could have emulated the warmth that permeated our spirits on that cold winter night. We immediately shook hands around our little circle and made introductions. I discovered that Daniel and José were also university students. Though each of us had arrived at this place with distinct backgrounds and circumstances, grace had now united us on a chilly snow-filled street. It was as though the shared language of our Hispanic souls had made a long-distance telepathic call, and had connected.

Now with the task of unearthing my immobile car before us, we proceeded to work together at pushing it out of its frozen rut. Common language and warm laughter filled the cold night air despite the fact that the job was demanding. In a short while we, laboring cooperatively, were able to liberate the tire of my Grand

Prix from the hole it had created.

After heartfelt thanks were expressed, followed by a final round of handshakes and calling out *"nos mantenemos en comunicación "*—as if to say we are here to help each other—my young family and I drove away from this hallowed site. I had found community within a lonely neighborhood and could now leave this place with hope. Hope that similar connections of solidarity would continue to create many more liberating opportunities such as the one I had just experienced. Even though the snow was still falling and the cold was intense, I felt a warmth of spirit as strong and incandescent as the Caribbean sun.

Raphael Falcón teaches literature and English at Goshen [Indiana] College.

Dreams of Light

a short story
by Gordon Houser

I think my sickness started with stomach pain, though I'd had headaches periodically since before we moved from New Mexico to Kansas. I'd wake up in the night with terrible cramps and run to the bathroom, lean over the toilet bowl and vomit. Soon my mother would appear and hand me a Kleenex as she rubbed my back with her hand. "What's wrong, honey?" she said at first. But as it became a regular occurrence, she grew more worried. She would moan an "Oh, no, not again," or else she'd mutter prayers like, "Dear Lord, have mercy," "Mother of God," "Holy Jesus."

I was happy that first summer in Kansas. For the first time in my life I had many friends. It seemed I came out of the wilderness to the promised land, an oasis of play. My mother and father seemed happier—my mother, I surmise, because she was finally close to her sister, and my father because he found steady work. By the next year, when my descent into hell had begun, that period of carefree play took on the aura of another country, almost another dimension. That boy who shagged flies like Willie Mays, slapped his bat at the ball, and ran the bases with abandon was another person, a ghost, a figure in a dream. That boy, visible to the world, became less and less distinct, faded in my mind into obscurity as the mist of my sickness took over my sight, and another world became palpable, a world of dark corridors and white uniforms, of soft moans and fearful screams, a world of impending death and the slow movement of time.

My first summer in Shannon, Kansas, was another time, one that moved quickly and now seems a blur in my memory. I know I was there, but my awareness of it is vague, distant, uncertain, like intimations a believer in reincarnation might have of an earlier life. My first nights in the hospital, as I remember, I dreamed about baseball, about exploring the creek for tadpoles or muskrat or some lost treasure more valuable than a discarded hubcap. Perhaps by now my dreams from those nights and my real life during that first summer in Shannon have coalesced into one reality. Who can tell which is real, which happened in my conscious mind or which in my unconscious?

My mother took me to a doctor, who prescribed some medicine and a bland diet of crackers and 7-Up. But the nausea persisted, and the headaches returned daily. I lived in bed, in a darkened room because the sunlight hurt my eyes. Back then, as I recall, I often dreamed of light streaming over me, a balm of brightness that did not sting my eyes or start my head throbbing. Thus my nights were filled with light, while my days passed in darkness. How long I stayed in bed at home I don't know. My parents had little money and no insurance, so going to a doctor was a last resort. My father had little trust of doctors. He'd say, "If they can't figure out what's wrong with you they'll make something up and give you drugs so they can take your money." Most of me agreed with him, for I feared doctors myself and had no desire to see one, but another part of me resented my father for making me stay at home, where I got no better. Despite my fears, I believed that doctors could cure most anything, and I suspected, though I never admitted this to myself, that my father cared more about his pocketbook than he did for me.

Eventually I returned to the clinic on Maple Street in Shannon, to a white stucco building on a corner across from the A&P grocery store. With no trees to shade it, the building reflected the bright sun mercilessly, so that I would walk blindly up the two steps to the heavy glass door, holding onto my mother's hand as she steered me into the air-conditioned waiting room. I had been there a few weeks earlier, before I got so sick, to get my shots for school. I sat nervously in the green vinyl chairs and looked through a *Highlights* magazine. Each time a name was called I jerked upright and thought, My end is near.

I was not too far from the truth. When I went into the doctor's office, he had me sit on a tall bed that seemed like a table, the kind on which Dr. Frankenstein created his monster. My mother stood by as the doctor squeezed my flesh, pressed against my stomach, pressed his cold stethoscope to my back, and listened to me cough. I remember the dark shadow of the stubble on his face and the smell of his breath, like peppermint masking cigarette smoke. "I want to take some blood and run some tests," he said. I looked at my mother, waited for her to say no. But she only nodded. I realized she had no power. She was as much a prisoner as I was.

I put on my shirt. My mother led me into an adjoining room where a nurse had me sit down on a chair with a desktop, similar to one I used at school. She took my arm, searched the blue veins for the best place to stick the sharp tube. I was crying, sniffling, trying to keep calm but failing. My mother held my hand, rubbed my back, kept saying, "It'll be all right, Ethan." And the nurse tried to comfort me with her lies about me being a big boy and that this wasn't going to hurt much. I was no big boy, and I was sure it would hurt. And I was right. I screamed when she pushed in the needle.

"Damn," she muttered, and pulled it out. "You're going to have to hold still. You made me miss the vein." She squeezed my arm, pushed it hard against the desktop. I held my breath, her rebuke having stopped my tears for the time being. This time she got it in on target. I watched the blood rush up the tube and begin filling the plastic container she held. The scene of my lifeblood oozing into a tube first horrified but soon fascinated my five-year-old senses. The pain from the stick of the needle had mellowed into a dull ache as I gazed at the spectacle with growing dispassion. By the time the nurse withdrew the needle and pressed a piece of cotton against the puncture wound, my tears had dried and I no longer even sniffled. This woman in white held some precious part of me in her hand, and I understood that my fate rested in that small container. I glanced at my mother, who smiled at me through glistening, teary eyes. But I felt a strange resignation. Like the blood that the nurse took from me, my fate was out of my hands.

I remember this feeling. I've had it a number of times since then, and I try to cultivate it because I believe it fits with the situation all of us face. Perhaps I simply felt relieved to be done with the ordeal. I remember looking at a calendar on the wall behind my mother. On it was a picture of a waterfall. For maybe the first time in my life I wanted to go home and take a bath, to wash the stain from my arm where the nurse had sterilized my skin, to just soak. I don't know why.

Ignorance was my aid. I never realized quite how seriously sick I might be. My greater fear at the time was beginning school. Even though I had made some friends—baseball buddies, fellow explorers of the creek—I remained a loner. I felt close to no one, kept my worries and wishes, my anxieties and dreams, to myself. Thus I did not look forward to meeting 20 or so strange children with pleasure or even indifference, but with dread. Since our trailer rested on the border of the catchment area of my school, Lincoln Elementary, only one of my neighborhood friends would be in my class. Then I learned that his family was moving to another state—Tennessee or Indiana or some other part of the nether regions outside my scope. Alone, then, I was to face the other children in my kindergarten class. The prospect terrified me.

But the detachment I had experienced that afternoon at the doctor's office gave me courage. Then, too, I had been frightened but had survived. And by retreating into some inner space of quiet, I had been able to remove myself from the pain and the terror. Perhaps I could use the same tactic when I went to school that first day. But I wasn't confident. This wasn't a technique I had perfected. I hadn't even tried it again. It might have been a fluke, a happy accident, blind luck. I didn't know. So my fears remained.

As it turned out, that first day of school was delayed, and when I did face it, the circumstances had changed dramatically—and not for the better. My first clue that something was wrong presented itself one afternoon. I had nearly forgotten the visit to the doctor. Relieved that it was over, I had turned my mind to other concerns: a coloring book I hoped to finish before school started, a war game scenario I had devised for my friends and me to play when I saw them next, and, always at the edge of my thoughts, the awful prospect of school.

My mother had gone somewhere and left me under the charge of my Aunt Barbara. My cousin Christine and I were playing Rummy when my mother returned. From my bedroom, where we had the red bicycle cards laid out in groups of three or more on the smoothed-out bedspread, a corduroy the color of an unripe peach, I heard the door open, then slam shut. I paused in my play enough to hear my mother sob and my Aunt Barbara gasp, then groan, "Oh no, Marie." More than once I had overheard my mother crying in the previous couple of months, but this was weeping, deep-down, heartrending, pain-in-the-gut sobs. I glanced at Christine, gave her an uh-oh look. She looked scared, as if we might be in trouble. Then she said, "Your turn." Her action was like clapping her hands over her ears to shut out the horrible news she might otherwise hear. I didn't blame her at all. In fact, I welcomed it.

While I tried to keep playing, I waited for the intervention, for my mother to open the door and give me the news. The news. I dreaded it. I wanted it. I thought, if I don't hear it, it isn't true, and I'm safe. Then I thought, will they try to hide it from me? My mind wandered, and I missed two opportunities to add to my piles of cards. Christine pulled ahead. "Boy, I'm creaming you today," she said. Usually I won, or at least it was close. And when she won, it bothered me—a serious setback in my world. But on this day it didn't seem to matter, and I felt myself drifting again into that resignation, the aroma of apathy.

It was not my mother but Aunt Barbara who finally interrupted our game. "Time to go, Sweetie." She spoke cheerfully, though I knew—and so did Christine, who gave me a sympathetic glance and, for once, did not argue about leaving—that her pleasant voice masked pain, that she had been crying, had waited this long to call Christine because she wanted to be composed, to not betray the horror she felt. "We'll see you around, Ethan." She bent down and kissed me on the forehead.

I must have frowned, but I wanted to push her away and yell, Stop treating me like a baby. In my way of thinking, anyone who could consistently beat a seven-year-old at Rummy or on his own capture 20 tadpoles in one afternoon was a fully mature individual. Another sign of "maturity": here I was, already masking my true feelings. This seems to be a major function of growing up—learning to hide what you feel, lying to others, telling them everything's okay when really you fear the worst disaster, or smiling at someone you'd like to strangle. Yet one more way that, as we "mature" in this society, we learn to walk in our sleep. And while we talk nice and hide our tears, we murder one another in our hearts—and in the process we kill ourselves.

When Barbara and Christine had left, my mother came to my room. She, too, tried to act calm, but it didn't last. Soon she was holding me, staining my hair, my shirt, with her tears. The blood test came back, she blubbered, and the doctor said I have leukemia. I had heard this word and knew it was something nasty, something worse than pneumonia, but I had not learned to associate it with a death knell—not until then. What my mother knew, and I eventually found out, is that being diagnosed with leukemia back in 1958 was like being given a death sentence. No one survived it. In spite of medicine's best efforts, it ran its course, and at the end of the course the person died.

I did not know all this then, but from my mother's sorrow I surmised that she was already grieving my death. I matured in that moment, played the adult, and sought to comfort her. I patted her on the back and cooed, "It's okay, Mom. I'll be all right." How many times in the next year I heard similar words, empty talk, as my parents, my aunt and uncle, nurses, the doctor, tried to make me feel better by uttering such lies. The irony, of course, is that their words, their frail attempts to bring comfort by saying things they didn't believe, turned out to be true. A number of these people, who with good reason expected to bury me within a year, now lie beneath the ground themselves. How fickle, how brief, is our life. A passing mist.

Ashton's St. Francis Hospital jutted ponderously out of an old residential area filled with large, impressive houses—three-storied Queen Annes, Victorian palaces—where Ashton's upper crust first settled but had long since fled to a neighborhood on the eastern boundary of the city. The huge gray edifice, a box of concrete with its many square windows, towered before me like a prison, I thought, when I entered it one windy September day with my brown canvas suitcase. I had packed my few baseball cards—including Mickey Mantle and Willie Mays, plus my own favorite, Dick Howser, shortstop for the nearest major league team, the hapless Kansas City Athletics—my weathered copy of *The Wizard of Oz*, and my toothbrush. My mother packed the rest—pajamas, I suppose, and other necessities I cared little about.

I entered the long corridors and met the stale, sterile smell of hospitals, an odor like ammonia over vomit that we associate with sickness and death. As the nurse led me, purposefully cheerful, to my bed, my tactic was to escape. My means were the book and the cards. I remember wanting to be left alone. My parents brought me there, and soon my father left for work, but my mother lingered. The nurse, I could tell, wanted her gone as much, or more, than I did. She repeatedly hinted as much: "He'll be fine, Mrs. Lamb." "We'll take good care of him."

I quickly grew to like that nurse. Though dour and sometimes harsh when some of us complained too much, she wasn't afraid of our illnesses. Like us, she had to live with them every day. To some extent she had to suffer the consequences of our being sick: cleaning up vomit when the chemo made us sick, or listening to one of us scream when the pain became unbearable, or waiting with one of us for news from the latest blood test. She knew, as our parents did not, that weeping and sentimentality were more selfish than helpful. She never offered us false promises. She never tried to hide the news of someone's death, though she did cry a little when she reported it. She knew that such news could not be hidden from us, and that once we knew, we didn't want to dwell on it. Bobby dead? Too bad. Okay, what's on TV this afternoon. A death was a reminder that our time was coming. We knew that. But for now we wanted to live as best we could, not think about what was coming. And that meant getting what pleasure we could, between shots and bouts of sickness, from our private storehouses, like my book and cards, or from the TV in our room of six beds. The staff carefully monitored what we watched, but that didn't matter. TV was new enough that just watching it was a delight.

I remember little about the other patients, my cell mates, as it were, on death row. Most of their names have slipped my mind. One, though, sticks with me. A dark-haired boy named Rick. He said little, seemed quieter than most. But one time he said to me out of the blue, "Ethan, I bet you make it." This kind of bold assertion, which we all considered meaningless from the mouths of adults who said such things all the time, usually to bolster their own hope, was almost taboo among us. At first I thought he was joking, but he rarely did. And his expression showed thoughtfulness. He meant it.

I muttered, "I bet you do, too."

He gave me a pained, incredulous look, then slowly shook his head. "No. I won't. Not for long."

Two days later he was gone. I asked the nurse, a Mrs. Johnson who told us to call her Erika, if Rick had died. She said, "His parents took him to St. Jude's down in Georgia. It's the best place around for children with cancer. But it's hard to get into."

"Is he gonna make it?"

She looked surprised, then sad. She put her palm against my cheek. "I hope so, Ethan."

Hope. We didn't usually talk about it with each

other. But each of us held onto it like a secret treasure. And Rick's words, his confidence, had sparked a new hope in me, though I tried not to pay it much attention.

Maybe a week after Rick left, Erika came in while I was dozing. I woke to the touch of her warm hand against my temple. "Oh Ethan," she said. "We just heard that Rick died."

"He did?" I became stiff, tried to shut down my swelling emotion. Then Erika pulled me against her, and I cried. The relief was immense. I could feel her shake as well, hear her sniff back the mucus of her sorrow. "I don't want to die," I mumbled against her shoulder.

"I know," she whispered.

I lay against her, her breasts a pillow for my head. I must have fallen asleep. When I woke later, she was gone. Other times, when the pain and nausea made it hard to sleep, I remembered her holding me, imagined myself lying in the lap of God. And the pain, the twisting knot that tore at my stomach, withdrew like a cowering pest.

Rick was only one of many. When I first came to St. Francis, the others in my ward greeted me across a spectrum of emotion. A few seemed delighted to see a new face, one more sign that they were not alone in their affliction. Others still seemed in shock, still looked scared, but welcomed me as one of them. Then there were three or four who hardly noticed me, their faces blank. They seemed to always be staring ahead or sleeping. I soon learned that these were the veterans, the long-timers, which meant they had been there more than a couple of months and were approaching their ends. At first I had felt they ignored me out of their hostility, but later I realized they had responded out of apathy, preoccupied by their own impending deaths. Within a week of my arrival, two of these boys died, less than a day apart, as if they wanted to leave together and not be separated long.

Most of us said little, and when the nurses wheeled out a boy who had died, the silence might linger for an hour or two. Bobby was the exception. He talked all the time. Some of us even called him Mouth. And he didn't seem to mind it much. He was heavyset at first, with round cheeks and puffy lips. (He got thinner, like all of us, since keeping food down was pretty well impossible.) I remember he had a scar across his forehead that I think came from an accident, when he fell and hit a glass bookcase. One of the guys had learned the word "lobotomy," so we would occasionally make fun of Mouth by calling him "Bobby Lobotomy."

Even though his chatter got on our nerves, it also helped relieve tension. Bobby talked about how mad he was when dinner was late, or he'd say how afraid he was to die. At first we told him to shut up. But later he became the spokesman for most of us. He was saying what we all felt but didn't dare mention. And once he said it, the power of those feelings seemed to diminish. We soon relaxed and let him talk.

Unfortunately Bobby didn't last long. It seemed like he was gone in a matter of weeks. It wasn't too long before I got to be a veteran. I began shrinking into myself even more than I usually did. My world became small, a space of three feet around my bed that I let certain people enter—Erika, my parents, my Aunt Barbara, one or two of the guys who were also veterans. I'd line up my baseball cards for ambience, then play an entire game in my head. I went through a World Series in which the Athletics came from behind to beat the Cardinals in Game Seven on a grand slam by little Dick Howser. The meek Athletics, against all odds, defeated their mighty opposition—David over Goliath, Ethan over cancer. The games exhausted me, and after each one I'd sleep. A good day was when I dreamed of baseball instead of being chased over a cliff or smothered by a blanket.

Then one night my dreams changed. It was winter. Wind rattled the windowpane, and a dusting of snow settled on the ground and the black branches outside. At first it was just an unusual dream. But it kept repeating itself. I'm sure there were variations, little details I can't recall. But I remember the brightness, a light bright as a ballpark but condensed into a shape human-sized. Sometimes I woke up when a nurse came in at night to check on somebody. She carried a flashlight or turned on a lamp beside a bed. The darkness around the bed shrunk back but lingered at its edges. The light in my dreams, however, filled the room so that no darkness—not a shadow, not even a particle—remained. And this was not the dull yellow light of a flashlight or a lamp but a dazzling whiteness—like pure snow, albescent fire, lightning that remains rather than flashes. Bright as it seemed, though, it didn't blind me. I hardly blinked, as I recall, when the figure of light approached my bed. I stared, transfixed but unafraid.

I'm dying, I thought. This must be what death is like. A boy named Mark told me once about a dream he had of being in a cave and seeing a light at the end. He'd walk and walk, but he never could get to that light at the end. He was convinced, he said, that if he ever reached the opening to the cave, he'd be dead. I think he told me about his dream in order to cheer me up, or perhaps to cheer himself up. But to me it was just another dream. And being stuck in a cave until you died seemed worse than being stuck in this hospital ward. Still, Mark's dream popped into my mind when this bright figure approached.

Am I dead? I wondered. I tried to speak, but my mouth went dry and I couldn't make a sound. You might think I'd wonder why no one else in the room saw this thing, but I'd forgotten about everybody else. Besides, if I'm dead, then I'm in some different, invisible realm. I can't recall any specifics about this figure, any facial features or length of hair. But I felt happily in awe. Ecstasy. I wanted to say, I'll gladly do anything you ask. But I couldn't speak. I couldn't even move.

The figure came closer, hovered over me. I heard nothing, felt no breath, recognized no smell, though what lingers in my memory—or perhaps I imagine it— is a faint air of mint kissed by a dusting of cinnamon. I stretched out on my back, my hands open, my palms up. The light, the brightness, the unquenchable soothing fire lowered itself onto me, and I melted, blanked out, died. I am dead. Gone. Free.

Then I awoke to the dull light of morning and to the sound of breathing. My own.

Gordon Houser is a writer and an editor of The Mennonite, *living in Newton, Kansas.*

Poetry, II

Gladiolus
by Keith Ratzlaff

There has never been a shortage
of places the body wanted not
to be: in the lifeboat,
at the awards dinner, under the tree
after falling, in the tree hanging,
in the box, in the box exhumed.

Or here in a photo on the inside page
of *The New York Times:* a skeleton
from the African Burial Ground, hands
folded across the now-collapsed chest.
A gesture, *The Times* says, meant
to help the spirit find Africa

again. And now scaphoid,
the wrist's bone boat, rides
in what was the heart's little harbor.
And cuneiform the wrist's wedge,
and semilunar the wrist's half moon
rises over the ocean. Remember

how often the torso was just bloody
cloth, the groin a red triangle,
the arms fired and set adrift.

That's over. Now fingers, wrist,
ribs, spine are mixed, all crossed,
all merely cups in the same cupboard.

But spirit you were right all along—
the journey is a map of the body.
Here in the backwash of the chest,
above the Inlet of the Pelvis,
north of the great and nameless
Os Innominatum, here at the sternum

you crossed your two lucky arms
at the middle bone called Gladiolus—
north of Ensiform, the false one,
south of the Manubrium—Gladiolus,
also called the sword of the body,
once called the wild iris of Africa.

Keith Ratzlaff is a poet and teaches at Central College, Pella, Iowa.

A Buenos Aires Picture

by David E. Leaman

A message about a message,
slipped under my apartment door,
in sloppily jotted Spanish.
Tired but hungry for something,
I sought the messenger.
Across the hall I knocked
for my phone-sharer.
The illicit splice bringing us together again.

With good cheer she welcomed me in
motioning I should leisurely stay
while she found the voice that spoke to me
some earlier time that day.

Retreating behind the bar counter to her machine,
a cabinet hid her countenance from me,
her legs also amputated.
What remained for me: a framed portrait
of a slender body trunk
moving ever so wispily as fingers pushed controls.

Her middle-aged visitor joined me near the door,
the rare meek *porteño* chatting
something about Thomistic education

and his cousin the political pollster I ought to meet.
Nodding I asked robotic questions
in which fractured language I do not remember.

Absent of thought I was held instead by the picture.
And the audible movements
of her back-and-forth tape.
Back and forth. Back and forth it went
searching the elusive—the message for me.
Fragments of various voices
whispering the gropings of a single urban day.

All the while her youthful body perfectly framed
by wooden and formica edges.
Her small breasts, snared in snug cotton,
slightly rhythmic as she searched.
Her sides and flanks naturally bevelled.
Nothing else visible.
Except her aroma breathing toward me with the stops
    and starts of the answering machine.

She found it then, the short message
buried in a pile of mechanized talk.
A British acquaintance of mine
speaking an idiom she could not discern,
inviting me to a party I would never attend.
Lucky for me I had not expected more.

She emerged then from behind her borders,
the rectangle emptied of its forms and small
    movements,
my strange enchantment broken.
Amidst the chaos of a Buenos Aires day,

WHAT MENNONITES ARE THINKING, 1998

I cared not whether it was painter or voyeur
who wished for that order and beauty a moment
    longer.

David E. Leaman lives in Chicago and teaches political science at Northeastern Illinois University.

Passing

by Leonard N. Neufeldt

If given the choice of bringing back
the lawlessness of their simplicity,
of boundaries poorly marked but closely watched
and bartered one at a time like stories
in the telling, would we bring forebears back?
And who first? the women? men? their children?
ourselves perhaps and places left behind?
Stories of lowlanders named after places
they'd worked for years into their hands
and feet, into each other's words?
Or what they would have been if nothing
were ever lost? if almost everything
is lost, although a better time was coming
and one shouldn't pack fears into tightly woven
willow chests and, like a stranger,
leave at dusk without wagon and furniture,
the unknown road eastward washed out
between the hills. Found again, it forked,
and at the fork a hymn bristled clean and cold
with words, stanzas of cloven desires
remembered as if for the first time.
Words bent and stiffened by the body,
known in the swale of our lives alone,
or so we thought, suddenly transpersonal,

WHAT MENNONITES ARE THINKING, 1998

news from a distant, double-bolted land.
Take this down: "It is night,
our feet tired as clay, flat and fearful;
yet we argue like family for hours
with border guards and the Registry
in the border town. We agree to change
our route but not our destination."

               * * *

It may have been the women who knew
what part of ourselves is ready
for the journey. Absence that feels
stones sharp underfoot, the inside
of the earth, grass, weeds, and path
gone from whatever happened long ago,
the present steadied by a name that changes
places at the table, the first-born's name
chosen once again, growing larger
within a third time, keeping her awake,
stirring oceans in her, unspoken words
turning the tide, watery body, marginal
patterns, and current together again.

The men know which armies, Catholic,
Protestant, are on the move,
positioned like goings-on of the day,
which villages, mills, millponds,
drainage canals will be spared, which
of the last hundred years have been too cold
for war, planting, or the old, which seawalls
will hold. Always strict business habits:
milk, despair, and the French clock
sold from the doorway, banter free of charge.
At table the father can't explain

his fear of finishing sentences,
a fear unphrased as his aphasic father's,
whose handsigns of hate for manifestos
and prisons became simple, then weak
as his left side turned useless beyond words
other than psalms much older than both of them.
Memorized psalms plain as the shallow coffin
open head to foot on a bench for viewers,
the coffin planed, nailed, and dressed in advance.
"My wife gave our children compassion,
my father and I have given them reticence."

Children, surer about stripling desire,
bring back from oblivion syntax of names
in scattered graves and separate graveyards,
buried sentences reappearing
entire or in part in sequence of stories,
surprising them. The heft of God
stepping back to let the stories by,
letting them channel breath through children
unwinding slowly like ferns into their shapes,
desires relearning the life they were given,
they gave themselves:
> Drie kleine geitele zatten op'n hek,
> zatten op'n hek, zatten op'n hek
> aan een mooie zomer dag.
The sun has set an hour ago; the children
are still on the fence, close together,
bent forward like huddled refugees,
holding the evening tight, singing
into the dark, the mist from the river
encircling them and the night.

WHAT MENNONITES ARE THINKING, 1998

Was weiter ihnen wird gescheh'n
Das ahnen sie und wir jetzt kaum;
Es wird den Kindern sein als saeen
Sie uns're Zukunft wie im Traum.

* * *

Because tellers who live by telling
may die with words hard on their tongue,
let reticence about the heart
collect all day on the barren curve
of the willow's silvered boughs to earth,
to the year's end angling down.
Birds banking out of the sky
and into it, the willow tree
a precinct for this coming and going
against the emptiness of air.
They scatter and disappear like names
returning, joining birds and air
to words of the song recalled, still there.

If singing ends the children's quiet,
let homelessness be their new start.
Let words join whatever departs
yet stays. Our coats much too thin.
The wind passing seeks our skin,
and through the skin our bones, but children
warm with smallness, sleep in our arms
as we sing to them, the sun warm
by the empty wall. One day children
will sing for us, their songs will soften
the difficulties of our love.

Leonard Neufeldt is a poet and professor at Purdue
University in West Lafayette, Indiana.

In the Museum of the My Lai Massacre

by Barbara Nickel

i. Plate

Sunrise burns like chilies,
shreds of cloud scarring
the mango sky. You
ignore it, stoke the fire,
poke your son's children awake,
ladle *pho* and the calm, white
noodles into bowls. Lam,
the youngest, sings to himself.
Slight as steam, his voice
stops when he sees you
listening. This is what you miss,
later, standing in the mess
of limbs, plate a broken
moon in your hand—
slips of song you almost
caught and kept unharmed.

ii. Hairpin

Her hair is blue-black swath
you comb with troubled

fingertips, unpin a cascade
of perpetual walks around
Hoan Kiem Lake where you must watch
lovers leaning into darkness.
All-night bus rides, jamming your arm out
the window, scent of jasmine left
on your cuff from the air curling past.

You kneel on a bed of blue mussels,
make a wreath from the shells. This takes
years. When you finish, she's slid
out from under it, hair
turning to dawn the colour of fat.
Her hairpin rusts in a fist.

iii.   Notebook

He skates on the frozen pond.
They skate on the frozen pond.
We skate on the frozen pond.
I skate—

He likes to make *frozen* last,
keep the *n* droning in that cave
behind his nose. But *skate,* pointed
as mosquito legs, escapes from
his mouth at *t* into pages soaked
with his whispers—whole afternoons
practicing English behind the well.
This morning he's come to school
early, repeats *What is your job?*
to squadrons of ants. A bullet
answers, and another. He falls
thinking these shots are stuck

syllables, stuttering, they can't
make words. In minutes he's dead.
The soldiers rest in ditches, hands
behind their heads. Wind
seeds the fields with his pages.

*Barbara Nickel is a poet and teacher at the University of
British Columbia in Vancouver.*

Eve of Change
by Kristen Mathies

*Women screwed up and ate the fruit of the Garden of
Eden and got themselves kicked out. As a result,
women make jello fruit salad for potlucks and men
run the church . . . it says so in the Bible.*

When she finishes this pronouncement
we all roll around on the floor laughing,
frustration and late-night giddiness combining
in an intense discussion of women's roles in the
    church.
We're all women in our twenties, and we're all tired.

When your house is on fire, how long do you stay and
    try to save it?
When you're being choked, how long do you reason
    intelligently with your torturer?
The bad is beginning to outweigh the good;
infrequent sips of honey
don't get rid of the sour taste in my mouth.
We agree on our dilemma: do we stay in the church
valuing its strengths
and trying to change its flaws. . .
or do we get out while we still can?

What the chorus sang was:
    No woman must destroy herself while fixing the
    world.
What I heard was:
    You don't hafta stay!
What I felt was:
    Guilty.

What kinda person am I, anyways?
Rage inwardly, speak truths with a harsh tongue,
but stay nice on the outside; don't offend, don't cause
    trouble.
Don't, for example, stand up and swear at the speaker
who proclaims the submission of women as God's will.
Don't set fire to each and every volume in the church
    library,
don't throw a hymnal every time "Rise Up O Men of
    God" or
"Onward Christian Soldiers" is sung,
don't kick the man in front of you who complains that
women are trying to take over the church.
And what kinda person picks fights with their own
    grandmother
about the equality of wife and husband?

My someday daughter will not have to feel this way,
I am determined. She will know, as I do, that
God is sighing sadly in her heaven,
waiting to see when the world will get it together
enough to recognize everyone's equality.

My someday daughter will be friends with the women
whose stories fill the Bible:

WHAT MENNONITES ARE THINKING, 1998

Eve, mother of humanity. . .
Esther, courageous saviour of her people . . .
Tamar, raped by her brother and crying out for
    justice . . .
Vashti, refusing to let her husband parade her in front
    of his friends . . .
Jochebed, outsmarting Herod to change the course of
    history . . .
Martha, rejecting the expectation that she remain
    silent . . .

My someday daughter will know how Jesus
was best friends with the women who surrounded
    him . . .
who were disciples and leaders and rebels.
She won't have to grimace in silent disgust
and vow to make things better,
because things will *be* better.
Things will be better because a group of women,
teenagers to retired people,
sit around a table at Archie's Deli and vent their
    frustrations,
laugh, eat pancakes, and plan for change.
Because people gather here and there, mobilizing
    resources
to show everyone what we already know:
That there is no room, not the tiniest space, for sexism
in a community that claims to be of God.

My someday daughter will be able to call herself a
    feminist
(the *other* f-word)

without making people suspect her motives and doubt
　　her spirit.
She will laugh in the face of restrictions
and walk past small-mindedness.
But someday is not good enough.

*Kristen Mathies is a graduate student at Wilfrid Laurier
University in Waterloo, Ontario.*

My Big Sister
by Christine Thomson

I said; I'm getting a bike.
She said; I'm getting a car.

I said; I'm checking out Japanese racers.
She said; I'm looking at BMW's.

I said; I like having my hair long.
She said; I went through that stage.

I said; I love Bergman films.
She said; He wears thin as you mature.

I said; I'm a department manager.
She said; I'm a mother.

I wrote her a letter that said she is
condescending and self-righteous.
She wrote me a poem that said
the same thing, but better.

Christine Thomson is a writer and editor in Phoenixville,
Pennsylvania.

A Longer Essay

Reflections on
20 Years of Peacebuilding
by Ron Kraybill

Reflecting on 20 years of experience in the task of building peace presents for me the question: Whose story am I telling—my own, or that of my community of faith? Central to Mennonite understandings of human life is the conviction that the web of existence is seamless, that individuals dwell in communities, which in turn are meant to nurture individuals. The Gospel is Good News only if it addresses both. Thus this account conveys both a personal odyssey and a communal journey.

Historical Context

An epochal story from the congregation in which I grew up, Bosslers Mennonite Church near Elizabethtown, Pennsylvania, sets the context regarding what I see as key understandings of many North American Mennonites about peacemaking in the post-World War Two era. Families in our church, farmers nearly all, resided on land that appealed to more than the locals. Situated near the Olmstead Air Force Base at Middletown within easy reach of the Susquehanna

River, well removed from dense urban populations but serviced by an unusual nexus of highways and railways, the gently rolling hills of western Lancaster County more than once caught the eye of military planners. In 1942 and again in 1951, the U.S. Department of War made moves to expand the Olmstead facilities by expropriating thousands of acres, including the fertile farmlands which families in our church had tilled for generations.

Both efforts came to naught.[1] I grew up on the story told by my grandfather, preacher Martin R. Kraybill, of a day of deliverance in 1942 when a delegation of community representatives traveled to Washington to meet with planners in the Department of War. As the delegation traveled to the Capitol, families from our church and others from the area gathered for a prayer meeting.

When the delegation returned that evening, they reported an experience received by Grandpa and many others as an act of God. The Colonel had been unrelenting. The nation was at war, he had maintained, many were making great sacrifices, and this community too must be prepared to do its part. However, as the group was preparing to leave a cable was handed to the Colonel which he read aloud to the group: "The congregation at Bosslers are in church praying right now for the preservation of their loved homes and farms." A silence followed, which was then broken by the Colonel. With tears in his eyes, he said, "Go home and tell the folks their prayers are answered. There is no intention of taking that site now."

---

[1] The particulars of the 1942 event are given above. Whereas the intent in 1942 was to build a massive TNT dump, the War Department in 1951 sought to build a $60 million expanded air base. However, the site was rejected for an air base due to the large number of sinkholes in the limestone soil.

That recent historical study has shown the actual sequence of events to be more complex than this account only underscores the world-defining role of this "exodus" event.[2] The story communicated many things to me and others in our community, beliefs that, as in most epochal stories, often resided beneath the level of conscious reflection. I still believe many of these things; others mark early steps on a journey in which I and others have moved a substantial distance.

Perhaps the keystone is the understanding that in the beginning is God and God's people, not government. The land was *ours,* we believed, to use for God's purposes. Government was the invader, an interloper driven in part by forces outside the realm of God's intentions which threatened innocent people. The military in particular was a threat. Alien and suspect though government seemed, Mennonite communities recognized the need for political structures to maintain order in society, even though in that era few Mennonites voted in elections. But as an institution openly committed to the organization of death as the ultimate response to conflict, the military to us represented something alien to God's best intentions, and we saw that it had enormous power to corrupt the constructive dimensions of government.

Alongside understanding the military as a particular threat to God's intentions for human life, this story carried another conviction: Divine reality may break in at the moment of greatest hopelessness, if God's people stand faithful in witness against evil. We knew, to be

---

[2] See Mary Jean Kraybill, "Bosslers Mennonite Church and the TNT Plant Crisis of 1942: The Making of a Myth," term paper on file at Menno Simons Historical Library, Eastern Mennonite University.

sure, from our own centuries-old canon of martyrdom that such inbreaking is never assured. Then too, the prosperity of the twentieth century had introduced a dimension of self-interest which surely tainted the motives of those going to Washington. Still, we knew in the end that we lived to serve God, not ourselves, and we believed that God would ultimately honor that commitment.

The story communicated other beliefs which I and many Mennonites have now left behind. Among them was the limiting assumption that peacemaking was primarily a matter of refusal to participate in war. Sectarian in theology and practice well into the 1960s, the majority of Mennonites were content to express their beliefs about peace to the larger society in negative ways during much of the twentieth century. The Mennonite Central Committee (MCC) Peace Section, for example, which until a decade ago represented the primary institutional expression of Mennonite peace convictions,[3] was established in 1939 in response to the threat of World War Two. It largely concerned itself for the next several decades with protecting North American Mennonites from conscription.

But the post-War economic boom of the '50s and '60s made Mennonites prosperous and ambitious, increasingly connected to the larger American society, and therefore more open to conversation with that society. During this time, the civil rights movement was introducing the concept of disciplined application of nonviolence to social and political problems into mass aware-

---

[3] The '80s and '90s have seen a proliferation and decentralization of Mennonite peace efforts to local peace centers, colleges, and seminaries, and greater prominence of peacebuilding as a theme guiding the larger MCC, as well as the efforts of various Mennonite mission organizations.

ness, a concept that appealed to that growing portion of Mennonites who sought a more activist way to express their convictions about peace. Equally important, the Viet Nam era presented Mennonites for the first time with a need to wrestle with how their understandings of peace differed from those of millions of others who also clamored for peace.

Thus the decision to establish the Mennonite Conciliation Service in 1979 represents the institutional expression of an awareness that had been developing for 20 years: To be peacemakers requires more than to decry violence. It also calls for active effort to remove the barriers that separate human beings and to demonstrate what it means in practical ways to believe that living peacefully with others is central to God's intentions for human life.

Early Personal Steps Towards Peacebuilding

My own movement into the field of peacebuilding began when I was a teenager in the mid- to late '60s as I heard tales of war protests and marches from my four older brothers returning home from college. I bade farewell to one brother who turned in his draft card and left to teach in Swaziland, uncertain if he could ever legally return to the United States. I saw a sister and her husband head for Somalia to teach for three years. I heard, read, and felt proud of accounts of Mennonites sending aid to the North Vietnamese as an expression of care for people said to be our enemies. These experiences aroused my interest in peace.

As a student at Goshen College, a Mennonite liberal arts school in northern Indiana, I sought out possibilities for a career in peace work. The only option for further study seemed to be Peace Studies, which focused on historical and statistical analyses of war, offering little that seemed relevant to ordinary people and small hope of employment as a field. Discouraged, I decided to explore seminary and enrolled at Harvard Divinity School (HDS).

Here, in my first semester, a radical Presbyterian, a former Baptist minister, and a pair of Methodists put me on the path to my current work. The radical Presbyterian was Bill Yolton, then Field Education Supervisor at HDS, who first told me about the field of "conflict resolution." "You know," he said in an early fall interview, "it's now taken for granted that many ministers get training in counseling skills through Clinical Pastoral Education (CPE). The same thing ought to happen to equip pastors for responding to conflicts. Why don't you go down and talk with Bill Lincoln at the American Arbitration Association and see if you can get an internship with him?" Lincoln was head of the Community Disputes Section of the American Arbitration Association in Boston and deeply involved in efforts to build black/white coalitions in response to riots over school desegregation in Boston. As a former Baptist minister he had hoped for assistance from the city's influential religious communities and was disappointed. "Penguins in white" was his sarcastic characterization of Boston area clergy who came and stood in the corridors of tense schools, courageous enough to locate themselves on the scene of trouble, but frozen with fear and clueless to act.

By Thanksgiving of my first year of seminary I knew that I had found my calling. I decided to use the flexibility offered by the Masters of Divinity program at

Harvard to create a self-constructed study in conflict resolution. Alongside standard seminary fare, each semester over the next three years I took a course in the larger university that related somehow to conflict: an introduction to classic Peace Studies with Karl Deutsch, a course in Social Psychology of Conflict with Herb Kelman, a seminar on Alternative Dispute Resolution at the law school with Frank Sanders.

One class project was convening a one-day consultation in late 1976 under the joint auspices of the American Arbitration Association and Harvard Divinity School to discuss the possibilities for religiously based peacemakers to assist in community conflicts. Yolton guided me to Jim Laue and John Adams, two Methodists who might be called the grandfathers of conflict resolution in the United States. Fortunately Laue lived long enough to enjoy some of the recognition he so richly deserved for his efforts. But his close friend Adams, who undertook conflict resolution initiatives under Methodist and National Council of Churches auspices throughout the '70s at places like Wounded Knee, Miami Beach, and Kent State, died of a heart attack in about 1984, largely unrecognized for his pioneering efforts.[4] Both came at their own expense to the consultation I organized, held at the National Council of Churches in New York.

Flush with the discovery of an approach to peacemaking that seemed relevant to ordinary life, during Thanksgiving break of my first year at Harvard, I was introduced at a wedding shower to Urbane Peachey, head of MCC Peace Section. I nearly dropped my

---

[4] However, Adams' experiences are recorded in some detail in his book *At the Heart of the Whirlwind* (New York: Harper and Row, 1976, out of print).

crackers and cheese when he began describing a proposal just then under consideration by the Peace Section to establish a Mennonite Conciliation Service.

This led to an invitation from the Peace Section to assist in consulting about this proposal as a summer assignment in 1977. For two exhilarating months I traveled throughout the U.S. and Canada, soliciting comment about whether and how to establish an office dedicated to assisting churches and communities in dealing more effectively with conflict. The answer was, by and large, yes. In June, 1978, a conference was held to enable further planning for such an office. In September, 1979, I began a two-year term of voluntary service as the first director of that office, a role which I held until 1988.

The Roots of International Interest

My interest in international issues also has roots in church and family influences in my childhood. Separated though we were from American culture by rural location, TV-free homes, and a profound skepticism of "worldliness," the families at Bosslers Mennonite Church were more connected to the rest of the world than many sophisticated urbanites. The executive secretary of the Eastern Mennonite Board of Missions and Charities, Paul Kraybill, attended our church and gave frequent reports of trips to Africa. My uncle, Nevin Kraybill, who had grown up in the church, was in Africa for most of my growing-up years. My father's cousin, the late Lois Kraybill Stahl, who had grown up in the church, spent her adult life in mission work in Europe with her husband Omar Stahl. Their son, John Daniel Stahl, lived with my family for several years during high school. Three of my elder siblings spent several years in Africa in development or education work.

I took my second year of college at Dag Hammarskjöld College, a short-lived 1970s experiment in international education in Columbia, Maryland. Living for nine months with 40 other students from all over the globe, including a month at the United Nations and a month in Japan, fixed in me a lifelong interest in international issues. A year later I took this a step further by taking a break from college and spending nine months living and working in Germany.

My experiences during the years of work with the Mennonite Conciliation Service provided another push towards spending time overseas in peace work. As director of the only religiously based conflict resolution organization at that time, I interacted extensively from 1979 to 1988 with people in the rapidly growing field of "conflict resolution." One consequence was that I came to more fully understand that peacemaking as I and my community of faith understood it raised profound moral issues whose full import could not be grasped except in the context of global awareness. Initially, the practical problem-solving focus, which then and now provides the common denominator in the field, had been highly attractive to me. It helped me to connect my desire to be a peacemaker to everyday problems in ways that neither my religious tradition nor the field of classic peace studies had accomplished. But increasingly I realized that my own understanding of peacemaking was rooted in deeper commitments than that of many in the field.

The most sobering and revealing moments for me

were the national conflict resolution conferences where, in the heat of struggles for recognition and turf, it became apparent that many of the professionals hustling into the field had difficulty practicing what they taught. Most memorable for me was the 1986 National Conference on Peacemaking and Conflict Resolution in Denver. On one hand I felt stimulated and encouraged by the intense commitment to peaceful resolution of conflicts apparently shared by a body of over 500 people. At the same time it seemed that many of the participants had only a superficial grasp of the concepts to which they so glibly referred. Ideas of "win/win" negotiations and joint problem-solving were frequently cited, but it seemed apparent that great competitiveness was at work among those attending. Participants guarded their training materials carefully. Prickliness among competing organizations and individuals became obvious in a number of sessions. I had the feeling that many were more interested in demonstrating their own success than in learning from or genuinely contributing to others. Perhaps most disconcerting, as an individual I felt drawn into the spirit of competition and egocentrism. Throughout the conference I wrestled with my own desires for personal and institutional credit for the work I and my colleagues had been engaging in.

I was scheduled to address a plenary session of the conference, and I decided to share my experience with the group as the core of my presentation. I confessed the inner pulls of competition and desires for credit and influence I felt, and observed that it appeared that these pulls were also at work among others. I suggested that conflict resolution is potentially more than a set of techniques, that it can also be a way of *being* with much to say about all of life, including the ways in which we function in our private and professional relationships. I closed by suggesting that as peacemakers we need to articulate our "theology of peacemaking," that is, to identify the values underlying our efforts in conflict resolution and work out ways to bring our lives and professional conduct into consistent service of those values.

I said this with sweaty palms and quaking knees, afraid that I would sound "soft," parochial and judgmental, and that my words might destroy my credibility in the larger professional field. Thus I was astonished after the session ended when many individuals pressed to the front of the crowded auditorium with words of deep gratitude. They too experienced the struggle I had shared and were disturbed by the dynamics present in the conference. For several years people continued to approach me in letters, phone calls, and at conferences to talk further about a theology of conflict. Some worked for religious organizations, but most did not. The majority were simply sensitive and thoughtful professionals working in secular organizations, people who had, through the course of their work in conflict resolution, come to realize that more was at stake than merely a body of skills and tactics. Most were not sure exactly what else was at stake, nor how far it could take them, but they were eager to explore.

Understood as a way of life, conflict resolution enters the terrain of some of the toughest philosophical questions of human existence. To assert, as conflict resolution does, that it is possible for human beings to resolve significant conflicts without violence contradicts a key assumption on which virtually all political structures of our world are based.[5] It is one thing to make such an assertion in an interpersonal dispute over children or boundary lines in a monocultural, middle-class American suburb. It is quite a different thing to assert it in settings where peoples are separated by ethnic or religious identities and generations of killing, where injustice is a central part of the problem, and where one group holds more economic, political, or military power than another.

As my understanding of conflict resolution as a way of life developed greater clarity, I increasingly felt that integrity and the frontiers of the field required me to spend an extended period of time in a place characterized by deep-rooted violent conflict and structural injustice. Only if I were willing to make myself, in at least a small measure, vulnerable to the pain of people in such a setting, through daily, long-term exposure to the realities they face, could I with integrity hold to the conviction that it is possible to work for justice and peace simultaneously.

Then, too, after nine years at the Mennonite Conciliation Service, I felt that it was in the best interests of that growing organization to be headed by a person with a different mixture of strengths and weaknesses than those of the founding director. Although my wife

---

[5] Conflict resolution practitioners differ, of course, as to how far cooperative conflict resolution approaches can go. Nevertheless, I think it safe to generalize that people in the field believe that it is possible to expand the range of situations amenable to nonviolent resolution of conflicts substantially farther than their fellow citizens commonly believe. To hold such optimism regarding the possibility of nonviolent resolution of conflicts so as to refer to it as a "way of life" (which by no means all practitioners do) is for me to assert that the principle of nonviolent conflict resolution is of more than utilitarian value, that it holds deeper status as a moral principal. It is the point at which this claim is made that conflict resolution enters the realm of difficult philosophical issues referred to above.

Meribeth and I contemplated Northern Ireland, the Middle East, and Korea, South Africa seemed to be the best choice. Mennonite Central Committee staff supported this, for they had sought for many years to work in the country and had been providing modest financial grants to numerous South African Christian "struggle" organizations. At their suggestion I contacted a well-known South African Quaker, Professor H.W. van der Merwe, who knew MCC workers in the region and headed the Centre for Intergroup Studies in Cape Town. Van der Merwe replied that they would be glad to assist if we came and offered a part-time research position.

During this time John Paul Lederach and I began a conversation about the future, which continued over the next several years. Our goal was to define our long-term vision for the ideal institutional base of operations for ourselves and, if they supported it, others that we hoped might join us. The components we wanted were: a setting where people worked collegially as an interactive team rather than as ambitious individualists; a mix of academic and practitioner work, so as to enable a sustainable blend of travel and home life, as well as action and reflection; and an opportunity to work closely with religiously-based peacemakers, particularly through the far-flung Mennonite network, without being completely defined by a religious institution. From this discussion, continued by my occasional visits to the States, by mail and email, and by John Paul's careful spadework with receptive colleagues at Eastern Mennonite University, emerged what we today call the Conflict Transformation Program and Institute for Peacebuilding.

For some time I had thought that unless I was prepared to spend the rest of my life as a traveling trainer,

I probably ought to acquire a Ph.D. If I had the degree, I could base part of my life in a university setting where I could train without living out of a suitcase. My personal desire, bolstered by my conversations with John Paul, fit unexpectedly with one South African reality. Whereas incoming church workers were carefully screened by the Nationalist government, we learned that university students attracted little interest. Thus I applied as a Ph.D. student to the Religious Studies Department at the University of Cape Town.

Still, it seemed unlikely that we would gain entry to South Africa. Mennonites had been routinely denied visas there throughout the 1980s, due, in part at least, to the extensive interaction between Mennonite development workers and exiled ANC members in Botswana, Swaziland, and Lesotho. Certain that formal ties to Mennonite structures would be the kiss of death for our mission, I resigned from the Mennonite Conciliation Service before applying for a visa. But MCC promised to provide us with a grant to cover travel and "settling in" costs, plus occasional living grants in South Africa if needed.

It felt at times like cloak and dagger work on behalf of peace, and we joked about being Mennonite undercover agents. The application forms from the South African embassy sought extensive information about previous employers, church affiliation, etc., and we struggled with how to truthfully complete these without flagging ourselves to computer-assisted South African security agents as "enemy." When I described our dilemma to Peter Dyck, feisty veteran of MCC relief operations in post-War Europe, he chuckled and said, "Remember Jesus' words, 'Wise as serpents, harmless as doves.' Never lie. Always tell the truth or you'll get yourself in trouble. But remember, you don't have to tell the whole truth!" On the application form, my "last employer" became "Conciliation Services"; our home congregation, Community Mennonite Church of Lancaster, became "Community Church of Lancaster," etc.

We heard nothing for months after sending our applications, and our planned departure date in late March, 1989, was rapidly approaching. In January I encountered Don Jacobs, a Mennonite with many years' experience in Africa who saw part of his current mission as circulating among American evangelicals. Hearing our situation he said, "Go see Piet Kornhof. I know him from National Prayer Breakfast meetings!"

Kornhof was the South African ambassador to Washington, a complex man ousted from a senior Cabinet role for being too accommodating to blacks, yet still prepared to represent the Nationalist government abroad, and he counted himself an evangelical Christian. Kornhof received us warmly at the Embassy in Washington. When we had laid out our desires to work with van der Merwe and contribute to peaceful change in South Africa, he burst forth, "If you are friends of van der Merwe it would be a sin against the Lord himself to keep you out of South Africa!" At the end of the conversation he picked up a phone and called the Visa Section of the Embassy in New York and asked that our visas be expedited. Within a week they arrived.

We landed in South Africa in March, 1989, in what turned out to be the dying days of the reign of President P.W. Botha. By September Botha was out of power, felled by a heart attack and replaced by F.W. de

Klerk. On February 2nd, 1990, de Klerk released Nelson Mandela and unbanned the ANC. Thus with a precision of timing that is difficult to attribute to mere coincidence, we received the priceless gift of being personal witnesses of the South African political transition. We cheered with tens of thousands in Cape Town as we heard Mandela's speech upon his release from prison and roared with hundreds of thousands in Pretoria when he was inaugurated as President.

Not only did I have the privilege of being an official election monitor with access to all polling stations, but as Permanent Residents in South Africa, Meribeth and I were able to vote! Between these landmark events we rode the roller coaster of do-or-die national negotiations. Along with our South African friends, we were filled one week with hope from unexpected breakthroughs; we were brokenhearted and fearful the next as violence repeatedly broke out and stalled talks.

Most satisfying of all, during the years when the future of the nation hung in the balance, I was able to work alongside hundreds of South Africans desperately laboring to establish what eventually came to be called a "culture of negotiation" so as to enable a peaceful transition to democracy. When we arrived, "negotiation" was virtually a swearword, for it implied willingness to tango with the devil. But the transition proceeded in the face of mountainous skepticism within the black majority who had lived with decades of dirty tricks from the Nationalists. People began to recognize that indeed their future might be determined at a bargaining table rather than over the barrel of a gun. Negotiating skills were increasingly seen as tools for constructing the future, tools required not only by national level politicians, but also at local and regional levels where new structures would have to be created.

From about mid-1990 onward, people with conflict resolution skills couldn't keep up with the demand for training workshops. Everybody seemed to want them, from white Nationalist Party members of Parliament on the one hand, to radical Pan Africanist Congress youth groups on the other, with local, regional, and national ANC organizers and progressive police officers somewhere in the middle.

Although my first love has always been mediation, it seemed clear that training should be my primary area of focus. For most of our six and one-half years in South Africa, I served as Director of Training at the Centre for Intergroup Studies, renamed the Centre for Conflict Resolution in 1994. Initially I conducted most of the training events myself, but as our staff expanded I trained replacements. By 1993 much of the training was being done by others. This freed me to work on special projects. Among them were: 1.) a series of workshops to introduce senior journalists to concepts and skills of conflict resolution; 2.) another to train election monitors in conflict resolution skills; 3.) another to train police officers in conflict resolution skills; and 4.) one to introduce conflict resolution and public participation processes into development planning under the new government.

Themes in Peacebuilding

What principles of peacebuilding have become central, over time, to my understandings of the task of working for peace?

First, my thinking has grown clearer and more

focused with experience regarding what I see as the ideal purpose of peacebuilding: it should be to support and empower facilitators of healing, not to do healing. Healing, of course, is the hoped for result. Our vision is to introduce a new way of living and being to the world, so we must focus on setting in motion processes that do not depend on external peacebuilders in order to be sustained.

Early in my work with the Mennonite Conciliation Service (MCS), I met with John A. Lapp, the incoming executive secretary of Mennonite Central Committee. "Your goal should always be to work yourself out of a job," he commented thoughtfully. I understood him to mean that mediators should seek timely withdrawal from conflict situations so as to encourage parties to develop their own means of working out differences. It seemed like good advice and I sought to follow it. However, as requests for mediation increased, I realized that it might call for a deeper forfeiture than I had first understood. I learned that as a peace activist I should seek to relinquish the goal of becoming the mediator and instead aim to mobilize others as mediators. Thus I shifted my priority to training mediators.

As demand for MCS workshops increased, it became apparent that a still deeper level of relinquishment was called for. The impossibility of training all the people who wanted and needed peacebuilding skills was rapidly growing apparent. Rather than training mediators I ought to be training trainers. I began pulling away from doing training workshops myself and sought to focus my priorities around developing others as trainers and pushing them into the limelight in workshops.

Even this focus eventually proved too narrow. The

greatest requirement of peacebuilders in our world is for more than training skills. It is for a broad and courageous vision of possibilities, widely dismissed as utopian, and for a capacity to mobilize others to live out that vision practically. Thus I have come more recently to seek to relinquish the task of training trainers. The "job," as I see it now, is to be an ally of those with a vision for healing who are present in every society and situation of conflict. I want to support them in finding ways to bring their dreams for creating institutions and networks of peacebuilders in their own context into reality.

This progression of letting go may not fit all situations. I still mediate, train, and train trainers, in part because I enjoy these things, and in part because I need to keep my skills sharp at all levels. Nevertheless, I find it a useful guiding principle that peacebuilders ought to seek to empower others to do the work of building peace. This often requires letting go of doing things we are good at and enjoy, to make room for others. Of course this is not always easy. Mediating and training satisfy deep personal needs for meaningful involvement with others. Every stage of letting go has for me come at some personal cost. Yet having made the difficult decision to withdraw from the limelight of one sphere of operation, I have consistently found that different, even more satisfying, rewards await in other spheres.

My own development has shifted, then, from an early focus on peacemaking as "doing events" (mediating or training) to "transforming and empowering people," and ultimately to building institutions. Leaving the Mennonite Conciliation Service was an important turning point for me in this shift, for it gave me a chance to step back from something in which I was deeply invested. When I ask myself what really endured from those nine years of intense labor, I realize it is not the number of mediations and trainings I conducted, nor the gratitude of conflictants in a successful mediation. What continues to leave ever-broadening circles of impact are the activities of a handful of people who heard and responded to a personal call to peacebuilding, due in part to their involvements with MCS.

Empowering others in peacebuilding is complex work. It is easy to fall into patterns in which the activities of professional peace workers empower themselves more than anyone else. The South African experience was particularly illuminating for me in this regard because, for the first time, I resided on the receiving end of overseas largesse. The number of foreign trainers offering to do workshops was an eye-opening experience. My response shifted from initial openness to skepticism and eventual irritation with having to constantly field queries from people eager to contribute to the South African transition.

Perhaps our greatest limitation as a struggling South African conflict resolution nongovernmental organization (NGO) was not a lack of knowledge about conflict and training, but rather a lack of funding for infrastructure to do things we already knew how to do. After a few experiments, I soon realized that even workshops conducted "for free" by overseas trainers cost us heavily in precious organizational capacity. Why should we tie up our staff organizing workshops for overseas visitors to lead when South African trainers were already under-utilized, due to lack of organizing capacity?

It also soon became evident that in the mix of motives driving overseas conflict resolution practitioners and organizations to seek involvement in South Africa, self-interest often overshadowed their commitment to South African needs. Few funders were prepared to fork over money to American trainers to junket abroad; they wanted evidence that U.S. trainers were seriously desired overseas. That meant that for their $1000 per-trainer-per-day proposals to stand any chance of getting funded, overseas organizations needed relationships with South African organizations like our Centre for Conflict Resolution.

Years of watching overseas organizations maneuver, exaggerate, and, in at least one case, lie outright as they courted endorsement by South African organizations for their training expeditions, made me a deep skeptic of my own kind—conflict resolution trainers abroad. Much was contributed by foreign trainers, I am sure, but I believe the dividends would have been higher had the money that went into their training and travel budgets been allocated instead to enable the hiring of South Africans.

Another dimension of the empowerment question is length of commitment and location of peaceworkers. Short-term visitors are powerfully driven to provide answers. They feel pressure to contribute something tangible, and they rarely have sufficient understanding of the local scene to grasp the complexity of the situation. It takes time to discover how ignorant one really is! If peacebuilders view their involvement as a long-term one, it is easier to avoid the temptation to offer outside solutions. Living locally is, of course, an enormous asset as well, for it not only enables far greater understanding, it signals commitment. We were surprised how much it meant to some South Africans that we bought a house in Cape Town. We learned that a South African speaking to a North American group of conflict resolution practitioners said, "If you want to work in South Africa, do what the Kraybills have done: buy a house and make South Africa your home for a while!"

In South Africa I came to appreciate that a great portion of reality as experienced by people locked in deep-rooted conflict has to do with fear and suffering. To have credibility in the eyes of such people, peacebuilders need to be connected to that reality in visible ways. This realization has moved the concepts of vulnerability and solidarity with people in conflict into a place of prominence in my thinking about peacebuilding.

On the other hand, I have also learned that the picture is more ambiguous than the paragraphs above suggest. Several years ago I spent a week in Thailand, under the auspices of Mennonite Central Committee, which sought to foster reflection about Thai approaches to conflict. Long-term MCC staff worked with several Thai partner organizations, who set up meetings in several villages so local people could speak of the conflicts they experienced and how they dealt with them. We heard deeply moving stories of painful, embittering conflicts, mostly unresolved. In a culture where public displays of emotion are unusual, storytellers often wept as they spoke. Driving home one day, the Thai pastor who had set up several such meetings and accompanied us expressed his great surprise at things he had heard. Although he had known these people for years, he had never heard many of the things told to us that day.

Sometimes people will say things to visiting outsiders that they might never say to people who are close to them because it would be unacceptable to do so. Similarly, I realized that six years with a South African organization was at times a handicap, for this made me a potential competitor in the eyes of some South African organizations. Outsider resource persons depart, leaving locals to move into leadership, whereas people living in-country raise the threat of displacing locals.

The key, I have come to feel, is the commitment of visiting peaceworkers to give priority to local resource people whenever they are available. Being a resource person, after all, is a highly empowering role, for it enhances one's visibility, credibility, and experience, not to mention, in some instances, financial status. Thus, being a resource person is an asset that peacebuilders ought never hoard. A question I ask in evaluating any invitation to work away from home is whether there are local people who could do the task I contemplate doing. Such a question may appear so obvious as to be trivial, but in South Africa it seemed that few overseas trainers asked it. It seemed rather that they reasoned: if an opportunity to train comes your way, grab it. The ethics of modern competitive professionalism take such reasoning for granted. But if our deepest commitment is to call people broadly to work for peace, I believe that we must consider all training activities in light of their impact on the empowerment of locally based peacebuilders.

Another major theme for me has been pedagogy. At

some future time, I suspect, historians will look back and shake their heads at the devastation done by methods of teaching currently viewed as normal. Small children are driven irresistibly to learn, but by the time they finish formal schooling, most have come to hate it. This ought to alert us that something is terribly wrong with accepted understandings of pedagogy. I believe much of that wrongness has to do with what Paulo Freire called the "banking" method of teaching, in which it is assumed that a few people wealthy in knowledge (teachers) possess what others need. Students are poor in knowledge (ignorant), and the challenge of learning is to transfer knowledge from rich to poor. This approach is devastating to self-esteem.

As a student I did well in some topics, but in others I struggled. I felt that I was not smart enough to master these topics easily; I often felt bored, and I felt guilty for not thriving. In short, I assumed throughout my formal schooling that any struggles to learn were due to my own deficits. Who can love an enterprise in which they are constantly forced to jump through other people's ever-rising hoops, and in which every struggle is implicitly framed as a personal inadequacy?

As my own sense of competence in the discipline of conflict resolution matured, I came to believe that the learning approaches taken for granted in most schools in our world are deeply flawed. For example, only as I began to write, did I come to see that the academic writers I had struggled to understand in college were often inept at communication on paper; my boredom and incomprehension were due in significant measure to the limits of their writing ability (I am tempted to say their laziness and arrogance, for good, clear writing is hard, time-consuming work that demands enormous consideration for the reader), rather than to my dullness.

Only as I began to conduct workshops did I realize the impotence of lecturing to enable learning about more than a small part of what people need to learn if they are to be peacebuilders. Only as a consequence of much experimentation as a trainer, bolstered by the influence of colleagues like John Paul Lederach, did I come to recognize that people have vast reservoirs of existing knowledge. If tapped in the learning process, these can bring a classroom to overflowing life. These experiences have made me passionate about good pedagogy. I seek to make this a hallmark of my work in the form of clear, unpretentious writing; in a practical focus in workshops; and in a constant effort to demystify things that, to people coming into the field, can easily look overwhelming.

Pedagogy is further complicated by the legacy of colonialism in a multicultural world. Conflict and appropriate responses are, of course, culturally rooted. What works as a peacebuilding strategy in one place may be disastrous in another. This means that efforts to develop peacebuilding skills must build on local insights, not transfer prescriptions from other places. However, conducting training outside one's culture in ways that truly accomplish this is extremely difficult, for although few colonial political structures survive, their impact on global consciousness remains pervasive.

When I am honest I must admit that there is a part of me that thinks I know what others need to know, that my way is better. That is not entirely bad; if I didn't believe that, after all, I wouldn't be interested in spending a lifetime trying to educate others about alternatives to violence. But a healthy vision for a reconciled world is one thing; cultural chauvinism is another. I suspect that many people in countries with a history of being dominated politically and economically by others would admit, when they are honest, that a sense of inadequacy or inferiority lingers. I have encountered among participants in workshops in post-colonial settings, powerful expectations that the trainer holds and should deliver "answers." No person who is committed to the empowerment of others—above all, no American whose cultural glitz dominates the imagination of the world's youth through radio and television—who packs a bag to "train" overseas can ignore this reality. Falling into disempowering patterns is as easy as falling off a log, and only constant vigilance can mitigate it.

In 1985 I was invited by long-term Mennonite Central Committee workers in Ireland to do mediation training in Belfast and Dublin. I taught mediation as I had been teaching it for several years in North America, a four-stage model for structuring face-to-face discussions. Concerned about cultural issues, I was at pains, I thought, to stress that this approach may not fit in all cultures and that it would need to be adapted to their context. Eleven years later I heard a presentation by Brendan MacAlister, director of the Irish Mediation Network, to an American audience. "Our Network had its beginning in 1985," he said, "when Ron Kraybill led a workshop in Belfast." My chest swelled for I had not realized that this active Network traced its roots so directly to my workshops. Then MacAlister continued.

"For several years we floundered as a Network and felt there was little we could contribute to the difficulties of our society. In 1991 John Paul Lederach came and did a workshop in which we looked at Irish ways of solving problems. Thereafter, we gave ourselves permission for the first time to deviate from the model of mediation we had been using. From that point our efforts really began taking off. . ."

While accepting credit for providing an important impetus to get the Irish Mediation Network established, I also had to understand that my inability to lead a workshop that truly empowered the Irish to acknowledge and build on their own culture cost them six years of precious time. Fortunately the commitment of Mennonite Central Committee to a long-term peace-building process ensured that this initial gap was corrected, as Lederach later brought an approach reflecting more sophistication in training cross-culturally.

The South African experience also illuminated for me the connection between empowerment, cultural issues, and a long-term perspective. Desperate at the rapidly rising tide of violence sweeping the country during the political transition, the South African political parties agreed to erect a massive national structure, the National Peace Accord, to respond to the violence. Heavy pressure existed for quick results, and the solution chosen was to quickly field as many trainers as possible. Along with many others, including a substantial number of overseas trainers, I booked my calendar full of training.

But when I look now at the training materials that I and others worked from, there is little evidence that they are grounded in South African experiences. In our haste to get something going, we grabbed the training materials available to us, and these were materials based almost entirely on American and European experiences. I would like to think that in the oral, experiential part of our workshops some of us took South African experience and culture more seriously than the written materials would suggest, but I suspect that, even here, we fell short. Developing responses to conflict that truly correspond to local culture is a slow, multi-stage task that usually requires several years to unfold. Haste and short-term horizons in peacebuilding almost inescapably lead to over-reliance on external resources and under-valuation of local ones.

Finally, a theme that has slowly worked its way to a central place in my consciousness as a peacebuilder is "community." Peacebuilding in the ways I have called for above places enormous demands on peacebuilders. To seek to make all training decisions, for example, in light of their impact on the empowerment of others may be an impossible goal for an individual peacebuilder who faces the demands of supporting a family. Our world does not yet value the skills of consensus-building sufficiently to make steady, income-generating work in the field easy to acquire. For the individual practitioner who has already made risky personal sacrifices to pursue an unproven career option, peacebuilding as I understand it may be both utopian and discouragingly judgmental. "Demand too much of people like myself," cautioned one friend, a gifted and deeply ethical trainer still struggling to establish a niche in the field of conflict resolution, "and the temptation to give up and shift to a secure profession becomes overwhelming."

The truth is that I couldn't have done the things I've been doing for the last 19 years had I been a solo practitioner. I depended at every step on the emotional and spiritual support, counsel, connections, and, by no means least of all, the financial largesse of a network of people scattered worldwide. This support has made it possible to adhere to a set of ethical standards, indeed a vision for what might be accomplished in human affairs in a world whose every structure erodes empowerment for peace. Peacebuilding as here described is only possible, then, as it is grounded in a community of people who share a vision of reality.

Painful and costly as I often find it to root myself and my calling in the Mennonite community, I have come to recognize that it is here where I can most fully engage in peacebuilding as I, rather we, have come to understand it. Life-giving approaches to making peace can come, I am convinced, from a variety of communities and visions for human life. But only as peacebuilders explicitly root themselves in such communities and visions can we offer true alternatives to the life-destroying visions which currently hold such sway in our world.

Ron Kraybill is Associate Director of the Institute of Peacebuilding and a teacher in conflict studies at Eastern Mennonite University, Harrisonburg, Virginia.

Book Reviews

A Muslim and a Christian in Dialogue by **Badru D. Kateregga and David W. Shenk. Scottdale, PA: Herald Press, 1997.**

Reviewed by Marlin Adrian

A Muslim and a Christian in Dialogue, co-authored by Badru Kateregga and David Shenk, is a unique and important book in the field of religious studies. The authors avoid following the ways of "least resistance" so common in other efforts at Muslim/Christian dialogue which either gloss over and ignore differences in order to project a facile and illusory commonality or exaggerate differences in order to inflame hatred and division. Both errors leave the reader ignorant, yet full of a false sense of assurance that finally the relationship between these two religious traditions has been revealed.

Kateregga and Shenk offer us a very different picture of the elements shared by Islam and Christianity as well as the very serious differences. Both, thankfully, are presented with barely a hint of the mind-numbing rhetoric representatives of both traditions are often guilty of spouting. The authors leave the rehashing of old issues in previous attempts at dialogue to the writers of the two forewords which precede this volume. These forewords, by Sheikh Abdulla Saleh Farsy and Kenneth Craig, not only help the reader catch up on the tone of previous dialogues, they also provide a contrast which helps even the novice appreciate the insight, compassion, and honesty which make the body of this book so refreshing.

The form of this encounter is meticulously fair. The spirit which emerges from the pages reflects a relationship between the authors based not only on mutual respect, but on genuine affection. It is this relationship which ultimately produces an exchange of ideas unparalleled in the scholarly literature and yet accessible to every reader, not only those with a formal education in religious studies.

It is significant that David Shenk stands firmly in the Anabaptist/Mennonite tradition. Of equal importance is his position within the portion of this tradition with a strong commitment to missions. Although belonging to this minority within a minority places him on the margins of Christian culture, the margin has the potential to be the "cutting edge" of inter-religious dialogue, particularly between Islam and Christianity. Many Christians who read this book will not only discover Islam, but, perhaps more importantly, they will be confronted by a form of Christianity that is both familiar and disturbing. That is, after all, exactly what the Gospel was meant to be.

Marlin Adrian teaches at Averett College, Danville, Virginia.

An Introduction to Old Order and Conservative Mennonite Groups by Stephen E. Scott. Intercourse, PA: Good Books, 1996.

Reviewed by Susan Fisher Miller

Conservative and Old Order audiences will presumably greet this book as a straightforward historical portrait, and that it is. Readers from the mainstream Mennonite groups may additionally find that it contains revelation and challenge.

The volume opens with a short "Introduction to the Mennonites." A simple diagram illustrates the points of contact, from 1693 on, between the Mennonite and Amish churches—including the formation of the Mennonite "Old Orders" beginning in 1872, and of Conservative Amish Mennonites, later called Conservative Mennonites, after 1910.

As John F. Funk and John S. Coffman introduced radical changes in the Mennonite Church, most members accepted change. But, Scott reports, some "saw the introduction of Sunday schools, revival meetings, colleges, organized missions, and English church services as an open door to pull the Mennonite church into the worldliness of American Protestantism. . . These scattered islands of conservatism eventually formed a loose fellowship known as Old Order Mennonites." Scott covers in detail all the groups who have come to be considered Old Order.

The Conservative Mennonite Conference is "historically much closer to the Amish than to the Mennonites," Scott points out. At the time of the Amish divisions in the latter half of the 19th century, some Amish chose to follow neither the conservative Old Order nor the progressive Amish Mennonites. They adopted aspects of both: the Sunday schools, mission involvement and meetinghouses embraced by the Amish Mennonites and the distinctive plain dress and German language of the Old Order.

In the Conservative churches, nonconformed dress has remained important, while mission outreach, historically viewed as suspect by some conservative Mennonites, has been pursed from the beginning.

Scott also describes the dynamic relationship of the Conservative Mennonite Conference to the Mennonite Church General Assembly. That relationship warmed in the 1950s and 1960s as both groups relaxed earlier restrictions on personal appearance and uses of technology. But since the early 1990s, due to caution over theological differences, the Conservative Conference has retreated from its rapprochement to the Mennonite Church.

Scott describes a second wave of Mennonite conservatism, which has swelled in the latter part of the 20th century in response to the larger church's move "away from conservatism in lifestyle and doctrine."

Scott's final chapter attempts to summarize the points on which most Conservative Mennonites agree: the centrality of the Bible, the importance of standards and discipline, the interdependence of Christian family life and education, caution toward technology and the appropriateness of modest apparel.

To the reader outside the Old Order or Conservative family, the book's information is revelatory because we know so little about these groups.

Intriguing discoveries occur throughout: that some

Mennonites drive buggies (so much for the progressives' efforts to remove that cliche); that Old Order Mennonite wedding couples serve wine and cookies to their guests (a nod to the biblical wedding at Cana); that the founder of Hershey Chocolate was a son of Reformed Mennonites; and that the Conservative Mennonite descendants of the non-proselytizing Amish have spread missions from Flint, Michigan, to Luxembourg to Guatemala.

Reading Scott's book brings the realization that we generally do not know one another.

This book also gives mainstream Mennonites the overdue experience of being observed as outside the norm. It is a strange and bracing sensation to flip from a modern photo of a plain garbed Old Order couple plowing behind horses to a 1990 shot of a crowd singing at Mennonite World Conference—baggy T-shirts, surfer shorts, Mohawk hairdos, and permanent waves dotting the audience—whose caption concludes that "many North American Mennonites have blended quite thoroughly into the larger society."

We are accustomed in Mennonite history to reading about progressives leaving behind those unprepared to change. This book, by contrast, shows conservatives staying a faithful course as the progressives impatiently romp off the path.

Learning more about the Old Order and Conservative groups might lead progressive Mennonites to think harder about issues such as conscientiousness, faithfulness, the role of Scripture and nonconformity—the supposed habits of our denomination. Increased contact, beyond reading about one another, might yield common ground and shared insight.

One notes with interest, for example, that when the first Old Order Mennonite groups were born at the turn of the century, issues of plain dress and mode of transportation—markers that outsiders rely on today to define Old Order groups as archaic—remained virtually moot. The points of contention were practices of worship and education—substantive issues that remain alive in all manner of Mennonite congregations today.

Also worth considering is that allegiance to nonconformity often led to the expulsion, rather than the voluntary departure, of those who resisted change. An area left virtually untouched by Scott, but surely called for in any interpretive follow-up to this volume, is the relentless presence of schism.

I was stimulated by Scott's chronicle yet abashed that so much of it came to me as news. For it contains, as surely as our mainstream histories, the perennial tensions of Mennonite identity.

Susan Fisher Miller, Evanston, Illinois, is an historian and writer.

A Community of Memory by Jeff Gundy. Urbana, Il.: University of Illinois Press, 1995.

Reviewed by Shirley H. Showalter

Jeff Gundy has found a way to bring Mennonite theology and culture into conversation with the "new thinking" in his academic fields of creative writing and literary theory. Other Mennonite writers, artists, historians, and intellectuals should take note.

The University of Illinois Press has chosen to inaugurate its series "Creative Nonfiction" with this book. "Plain fact transformed into art" is the way the press itself describes the "burgeoning genre" called "creative nonfiction." Many other labels might be as accurate—for example "postmodern novel." By using multiple narrators, blurred boundaries between forms, a non-linear plot, and multiple perspectives on history, Gundy's book blends some of the elements of the novel with some elements of postmodernism in other art forms.

Reading *A Community of Memory* is like viewing a deconstructed house with the plumbing and wiring visible on the outside. Gundy uses the first-person author-narrator's voice in italics throughout the text. He also enters into the lives of his other characters, most of whom are his own Amish and Mennonite ancestors. These multiple narratives allow the reader to reflect upon the nature of selfhood and the relationship of story to identity. Along the way, Gundy's lyric descriptions play a descant over the sometimes pious and often irreverent hymn he raises to land, language, and community.

In this his first book of prose, which follows the publication of more than 150 poems, Jeff Gundy establishes himself as peer within a wide circle. Inspired by the late William Stafford, Gundy sometimes sounds like Scott Russell Sanders or Annie Dillard or Wendell Berry. But he also sounds very much like a Mennonite in conversation with other U.S. Mennonite poets, especially Julia Kasdorf and Jean Janzen. Surely the Mennonite "Renaissance" (a misnomer, perhaps, but nevertheless one with precedent, such as the name "Harlem Renaissance") which began among Canadian Mennonite writers in the 1960s and '70s has worked its way south.

A second postmodern feature, the blurring of literary genres, gives Gundy the opportunity to explore many kinds of boundaries and the spaces between them. By blurring the boundaries between literary forms, Gundy can look for interstices—the places where his people and his vocation of writing can come together. To cite one example out of many: *"George and Clara* [Gundy's grandparents] *were back there over the borderline where life becomes History, memorable, every salvaged scrap imbued with meaning and historical significance like bread soaked in wine, or grape juice]* (102). In his effort to construct meaning out of scraps of memory, Gundy discovers that the images he brings back have the power to haunt him, to challenge his own lack of borders: *"I was so broadminded I sometimes wondered if I had any borders at all. I was impatient and sarcastic and an intellectual snob . . ."* He begins to resent the incessant goodness of his ancestors, but he also feels their power to challenge him on a personal, not just literary, level: *"It made me feel like I should change my life, start being kinder to strangers, quit feeling superior and sarcastic all the time."*

With these words Gundy has entered dangerous territory for a poet. No modernist would write like this. But Gundy is not a sentimentalist either. He concludes the paragraph above with these words: "Surely there must be more to it than that" (103). There is more to it than that. Throughout the book the tension between "filial piety," Gundy's "stylishly nihilistic buddies" in the literary world, and a problem Gundy calls "my own inability to maintain seriousness" (or what Simone Weil might call his lack of attention) is the real subject.

Because this book does not depend upon a traditional linear plot structure, it may be hard for some readers to follow. This lack of clearly defined beginning and ending is another characteristic of the postmodern novel. Gundy's voice changes as he moves from character to character, male and female, old and young. The narrator voice alternates between third-person description, direct address to the characters, and direct address to the reader, sometimes with timidity, sometimes with conviction. The only voice in the book that does not belong to a Gundy blood relative is that of renegade Amish poet Joseph Joder. His story comes in the middle of the book, a pivot point, but not the traditional "denouement." We continue to feel Joder's unnamed "godfather" presence as we continue to read. The book aggregates its power rather than releasing it. The characters are more like the pilgrims of *Pilgrim's Progress* or *The Canterbury Tales* than they are like the alienated individuals in *The Sun Also Rises* or *The Great Gatsby.*

The echo of pre-modern form and pre-modern values is the fourth postmodern feature of the book. Architectural historians use the term "doublecoding" to refer to works that contain more than one time period. The purpose of the stories from the past is not to reify the old but to stimulate the new. Gundy forces the old to have conversation with the new either through ironic distance or through the autobiographical, italicized musings of his authorial voice. At the end of the book, Gundy brings poet/critic Robert Hass into his story and describes his own attraction to Hass's poems, one of which he quotes. He allows the other poet to make his case—that the placement of memory in words is the only solace the poet, or anyone, can have, because "all the new thinking is about loss."

Gundy does not rush to attack this idea. In fact, he allows it to stand on its own merit and appreciates its potency. Like Hass, Gundy finds language inadequate to describe what he wants to say: "It's hard to explain exactly." But unlike Hass, he is not content to let the matter rest with mere words. He goes on to tell a story about what happens at a family reunion:

We stay in comfortable lodges, take the kids swimming, walk the trails, and on Sunday morning we gather to sit together, report on our jobs and our children, reminisce and speak for the ages for an hour or so. My father always tries to say how humbled and impressed he is by what the next generation, my generation, has done and is doing. He's a fine farmer and a father I'm proud of, but a man not easy with words or in front of an audience, and he always ends up stumbling and then stopping. The words fail him as they do all of us in the end, and he wipes his eyes a little and laughs a little and somebody else picks it up or somebody's child starts crying. But we know what he means to say. All the new thinking is not about loss.

Jeff Gundy is his father's son, not only in what he says, but in what he doesn't say. The flaws of the book consist of occasional lapses of diction. The triumph of the book lies in what Willa Cather liked to call "the thing not spoken."

The genuine humility of the author's voice is matched only by the grandness of his aim.

Shirley H. Showalter is president of Goshen (Indiana) College.

No Longer Alone: Mental Health and the Church by
John Toews with Eleanor Loewen. Waterloo, ON,
Scottdale, PA: Herald Press, 1995.

Reviewed by Anne-Marie Klassen

This book represents the meeting of two traditional-
ly very separate realms: mental health and the church.
Ironically, as people search for balance and truth in
their lives, they have often been discouraged from
either exploring their Christian faith or seeking the
help of mental health professionals. In this book Toews
and Loewen integrate faith and mental illness.

Toews is a psychiatrist, currently a faculty member
at the University of Calgary. He provides the knowledge base for the understanding of mental illnesses and
invites readers to accept this understanding in the context of their Christianity. He accomplishes this by using
Scripture throughout the text, paralleling experiences,
emotional states, and interactions of Biblical figures to
present-day occurrences. The titles of chapters address-
ing anxiety disorders, mood disorders, and addictions
are verses from the Bible. This frames the topics in a
new and different light, capturing the essence of these
issues.

Loewen is currently a faculty member at Catherine
Booth Bible College and has an extensive background
in education. With the use of her skills as an adult education specialist, Loewen's contribution is apparent in
the organized and focussed layout of the material.

The chapters generally begin with Scripture text,
opening thoughts, a story, a focus section, followed by
a search section. As the book is designed to be a study

guide, for either personal or group work, questions for further study and additional resources are included at the end of each chapter. This is valuable, since Toews gives only a brief treatment of the topic. Further study and discussion is necessary within the church in order that its role becomes clear.

Generally the presentation of the material is clear, with concise explanations of psychiatric and theological terms. The content flows logically from the initial questions of what mental health is and the life stages of the Christian faith. These first few chapters provide the background for the more complex subjects of "Who Sinned?" and "The Need for Healing." Exploration of sources or causes of mental illness and the spiritual component of healing—"to restore to wholeness"—are addressed.

A shift to a focus on emotions and responses to life events gently moves the text toward the review of specific mental disorders. Several chapters briefly describe panic disorder, generalized anxiety disorder, depression, and schizophrenia. The basic information is good, but greater detail and further study are required to fully comprehend and to respond in a helpful manner to persons with such illnesses. The sketchy accounts of some of the disorders tend to present a simplistic view and to minimize the severity of the disorders and their impact on daily life.

The final chapter deals with the stigma of mental illness and how society perpetuates this false view. In the context of how Jesus challenged stigma, as he ate with tax collectors and spoke to women as equals, the question of how the church should interact with people with mental illnesses becomes easier to answer.

Practical suggestions for individuals and groups are included in the final pages of the book.

The value and use of this book cannot be more strongly emphasized and recommended. The blending of psychiatry and Christianity is initially frightening, as it has been so seldom addressed openly in the potentially caring and supportive community of believers. Toews writes clearly and directly about fears and the individual as follows: "Like all things, once we start to understand them, fears decrease. Fears are largely based on the unknown. We begin to see people who struggle with these difficult disorders in a different light. We see them as people first."

Anne-Marie Klassen is a writer in Winnipeg, Manitoba.

I & II Thessalonians (Believers Church Bible Commentary, Vol. 7) by Jacob Elias. Scottdale, PA: Herald Press, 1995.

Reviewed by Charlotte Holsopple Glick

Pastors and congregations today struggle with issues of accountability, sexual immorality, exercising of spiritual gifts, and the role of leadership. The early church at Thessalonica also wondered how to understand its current situation and comprehend "the day of the Lord."

Today, we encounter many approaches for sharing the gospel of Jesus Christ within a culture bombarded by the mass media and the high-tech worldwide web. Paul and his missionary companions "merely" wrote letters.

What can pastors and congregations today learn from these letters? Jake Elias invites readers—inexperienced and experienced pastors, untrained and trained congregational leaders, and novice and mature believers—to "listen in."

The text and commentary resound with emphasis that the "day of the Lord" will come in glorious array to complete the life, death, and resurrection of Jesus Christ. God's people are an essential ingredient in the process of bringing shalom to this world. It should be no surprise that God has allowed words to be scribed by Paul and others that still hold relevance and contemporary courage and challenge. By presenting this material in very understandable language on various sides of the scholarly debates, Elias is clear that we hear the messages from a believers church perspective.

His method of pulling apart the passages in sentence-flow diagrams allows readers to hear the whispers of the text amid the loud resounding themes of faith and practice. Listen in and you will hear.

Charlotte Holsopple Glick, Goshen, Indiana, is a conference minister in the Mennonite Church.

Anabaptist History and Theology: An Introduction by C. Arnold Snyder. Kitchener, ON: Pandora Press, 1995.

Reviewed by John D. Roth

During the past 50 years or so, the historiography of the Anabaptist movement has undergone several profound transformations. At mid-century, Harold S. Bender and his generation of colleagues at Goshen, Indiana and Bethel, Kansas challenged the caricature of Anabaptists as wild-eyed, politically seditious fanatics—a commonplace assumption in Reformation scholarship, with roots going all the way back to Martin Luther—and argued instead that the Anabaptists were Bible-centered pacifists, courageous followers of Jesus and the dictates of their religious consciences, even to a martyr's death. Purged by Bender of its most extreme elements, Anabaptism—especially of the Swiss Brethren variety—became a new standard of Christian faithfulness within the Mennonite Church, an important source of denominational identity and renewal. At the same time, scholars in the wider academy, such as Roland Bainton, Franklin Littell, and George Williams, granted legitimacy to this heroic reading of the Anabaptist movement beyond Mennonite circles: in their publications, the Anabaptists were forerunners of such mainstream and modern notions as religious volunteerism, the separation of church and state, and the freedom of the individual conscience.

Since then, however, our understanding of the Anabaptist movement has become considerably more nuanced, more complex, and, not surprisingly perhaps, more fragmented. In the mid-1970s, a new generation of scholars—trained primarily in the disciplines of intellectual and social history—discovered in their reading of the archival records a multiplicity of movements advocating radical reform in the sixteenth century. Scholars in the so-called "polygenesis school" emphasized the wide-ranging theological and ecclesiological diversity among groups practicing believers' baptism; they raised new and troubling methodological questions about scholarly objectivity and the appropriate relationship between religious and disciplinary commitments; they insisted that the language of religious reform was rooted in a social context, shaped at least as much by the Peasants' War, popular anticlericalism, or eschatological expectations as by a simple reading of the New Testament; and, above all, they challenged the notion of a "normative" or "evangelical" Anabaptist movement, preferring instead to catalog and to analyze the bewildering variety of nonconformist leaders and radical causes.

But like all scholarly fashions, the polygenesis approach also reached a point of diminishing returns. Though essays continued to use the term "Anabaptism," the meaning of the word gradually lost most of its conceptual usefulness. As a distinct or coherent movement, Anabaptism had virtually disappeared in the scholarly literature—swallowed up into vague and general categories like anticlericalism, or forgotten in a host of extremely specialized monographs devoted to nuances of intellectual influence or the quotidian details of biographical narratives.

All this is a long introduction to the book at hand. But one cannot fully appreciate the audacious scope of

Arnold Snyder's new volume, or the imaginative verve of its conceptual approach, without some understanding of the broader historiographical context. Snyder fully understands the polygenesis critique of the "Bender school." He knows, for example, that every text reflects a context, that theological ideas are inseparable from their social settings; he is aware that Anabaptism did not appear *ex nihilo* and that the Anabaptist movement embodied considerable theological variety from the very beginning; he is a trained historian, steeped in the archival sources, sensitive to the methodological debates regarding objectivity and commitment.

Yet at the same time, Snyder boldly insists that amidst all the variety of radical reforms in the sixteenth century one can still discern common features of a distinctive movement that can properly be called "Anabaptist." He refuses to flinch from the daunting challenge of describing this movement, threading complex theological themes into the fabric of specific socioeconomic contexts while simultaneously telling the unfolding narrative of individual leaders and specific groups. And, perhaps most provocatively, he even suggests that the story of Anabaptist history and theology—told honestly, in all its folly and all its glory—might be relevant to twentieth-century believers.

In Snyder's own words, *Anabaptist History and Theology* attempts to "provide a fairly concise narrative describing the birth and evolution of the sixteenth century Anabaptist movement." To meet that goal, Snyder organizes his material into four major sections of unequal length. The first, entitled "Context of Reformation and Radical Reformation," highlights the various streams of radical social and religious critiques—including Thomas Müntzer, Andreas Karlstadt, Caspar Schwenckfeld, and the Peasants' War of 1525—which not only influenced, but also sustained, the early Anabaptist movment in Switzerland, Strasbourg, and South Germany.

The second section—"The Setting of Initial Boundaries: 1525-1540"—traces the emergence of Anabaptist congregations in Switzerland, South Germany/Austria, Strasbourg, and the Netherlands. Topical chapters on such themes as Anabaptist hermeneutics, the communication of Anabaptist ideas, and the "core" of an emerging Anabaptist theology punctuate more traditional narrative summaries of the Anabaptist movement in various geographical regions.

Snyder then elaborates on these basic themes in greater detail and nuance, pushing them forward chronologically, in the third and longest section, "The Development of Anabaptism, 1525-ca. 1600." Here he describes the intramural discussions (and disagreements) within and among various Anabaptist groups, focusing on political themes (the sword, the oath, Münster and its aftermath), socio-economic issues (mutual aid, egalitarianism, marriage), and theological questions and religious reform (spiritualism, discipline, and ecclesiology).

A brief concluding section suggests the process by which the inner dynamism of the early movement gradually adopted the more rigid boundaries of an established sect. In an epilogue Snyder addresses the difficult question of the relevance this history might have for the contemporary believers' church. The volume includes six maps and 29 illustrations, along with a selected bibliography and an index. A review of Anabaptist historiography appears as an appendix.

For readers deeply interested in the Anabaptist movement or the radical reformation in general, there is much to recommend in this book. Snyder offers a coherent narrative of the basic Anabaptist story which takes into account the most recent scholarship while advancing at the same time a fresh reading of the sources. In his telling, pneumatology—that is, encounters with the Holy Spirit and subsequent reflections upon the meaning and the consequences of those encounters—emerges as the central theme of the story, the thread which binds together all of the various centrifugal elements. Beyond a shared commitment to some form of believers' baptism, the thing that pulled such diverse figures as Thomas Müntzer, Hans Denck, Balthasar Hubmaier, Michael Sattler, Pilgram Marpeck, Jan van Leiden, and Menno Simons into a common conversation, he suggests, was a deep, creative tension between the *inner* and the *outer* Word. In hermeneutics, this tension took the form of a debate between spiritualist and literalist readings of Scripture; in ecclesiological discussions, it expressed itself in disagreements over the visible church vs. the invisible church, and related struggles to define the boundaries of the visible church through the use of church discipline and the ban. But the "heart and soul of the Anabaptist movement," according to Snyder, "is found in its soteriology," a view of salvation which linked the inner working of the Spirit of God (*Gelassenheit,* grace) with the outer expression of the spirit in regenerated lives of obedience and discipleship.

One obvious strength of Snyder's work is his interest

in extending the story of the Anabaptist movement beyond the first generation. Over time, and particularly in the wake of the debacle at Münster, a reaction against an excessive pneumatic emphasis—of both the spiritualist and the apocalyptic variety—sets in, leading to a greater emphasis on Biblical literalism, hierarchical leadership, church discipline, and the ban. Snyder details the process by which various, sometimes competing, theological traditions emerged among the heirs of the radical reformers.

Another expression of Snyder's originality can be found in his chapters on oral communication, Anabaptist understandings of marriage, and the role of women in the Anabaptist movement. Though much of the book synthesizes the scholarship of others, here the author makes a genuinely original contribution to the broader discussion, demonstrating that archival fields already plowed by generations of scholars can still yield fresh insights.

Anabaptist History and Theology is not a perfect book. Specialists in various fields will undoubtedly want to quibble with any number of Snyder's general arguments. I found myself wondering, to cite only one small example, why the group which gathered for a short period around the leadership of Pilgram Marpeck did not survive. At several key points in the argument, Snyder suggests the Marpeck's conciliatory approach to contentious issues—on the question of the Christian magistracy, for example, or the tendency toward perfectionism in some Anabaptist teachings on regeneration—offers a theological *via media* which modern readers should seriously consider. But he never addresses the question of why Marpeck's theological perspectives failed to produce a viable church or a sustained tradition, a question which clearly is of both historical and contemporary interest.

Snyder also, at times, seems a bit uncertain of his intended audience. He states in the preface that he wants the volume "to be accessible to university students," but he also hopes it will have "something to say to people in the churches." And indeed, for the most part he successfully bridges these two groups. Yet there is also a sense that this book is really a penultimate draft, still awaiting the rigorous pen of the copy editor. The topical chapters on marriage, economics, hermeneutics, or women—excellent in their own right—tend to disrupt the narrative flow of the argument. There is an organizational tendency, especially in later chapters, to revert to the encyclopedic format of George Williams's *The Radical Reformation* or to thematic lists of theological topics or themes in which sub-headings are not always clearly distinguished from main headings. At its best, one has the sense of witnessing a skilled juggler at work, somehow managing to keep an amazing number of moving balls in the air at the same time; at its worst, the labored exertions of the juggler can distract one's attention from the artistry of the craft.

All the same, the scope and erudition of this book set a new standard for Anabaptist studies. It offers a masterful survey of the latest scholarly literature while simultaneously providing an original and creative synthesis. It tells the sweep of the Anabaptist story in a way which respects the genuine pluralism within the movement while highlighting the common themes. And along the way the author suggests, tactfully and subtly, that the history of the Anabaptist movement continues to have ongoing relevance for the contemporary heirs of that tradition.

"Art, like morality," G.K. Chesterton once wrote, "consists in drawing the line somewhere." Arnold Snyder has taken a bold step in this volume by drawing some lines, by suggesting that there is indeed such a thing as an "Anabaptist" history and theology. Even if readers do not agree with his finding and argue that the lines should be drawn elsewhere, they will need to do so in conversation with this book. By opening a new forum for discussion, Snyder has done scholarship and the church a great service.

John D. Roth is the editor of Mennonite Quarterly Review *and teaches history at Goshen (Indiana) Collge.*

Prayer Book for Earnest Christians, translated and edited by Leonard Gross. Scottdale, Pa.: Herald Press, 1997.

Reviewed by Gerald Studer

Harold Bender's statement in the *Mennonite Encyclopedia* (1959, vol. 4, p. 211) that "English-speaking American Mennonites have never produced nor used prayer books in public worship, and seldom, until recent times, in private or family worship" has been true all too long. Consequently none of the historic Dutch Mennonite or German Mennonite prayer collections had ever been translated into English until now. After 57 German editions of this prayer book in North America, which have enabled continuous use among the Amish, finally this reservoir of prayers for many different occasions has become available for the enrichment of English-speaking Christians as well.

This first complete and self-contained prayer book for Mennonites is most likely of Palatine origin. In general, Mennonites have always practiced free, extemporaneous prayer at church and at home. However, after 1600, Dutch Mennonites felt a need for printed prayers, mainly for home and private devotions, and a few short collections of such prayers were published.

Not until 1708 did the Swiss-origin Mennonites in South Germany take the decisive step of producing a complete prayer book of their own, *Die Ernsthafte Christenpflicht,* which has now been skillfully translated into English. The original work contained only 36 prayers—two for every day, five for times of temptation and anxiety, and 29 general prayers. Later editions increased the number of prayers, including prayers for church services and other occasions, thus changing the character of the book.

These prayers address a wide variety of situations— a plea for Christian virtues or for those who are suffering, a petition against schism or on behalf of those fallen from fellowship, or prayers for political authorities and enemies. The later editions added prayers for a traveler, for unity of mind and understanding, for those depressed, for use with baptism or the Lord's Supper, and for those about to be married. Intermingled are prayers before a meal, of parents for their children, for before or after a funeral, for faithful laborers in the Lord's harvest, and even for comfort during physical poverty.

This collection is comprised of prayers, both by Mennonites and non-Mennonites, some of which were rephrased, extended, or simply copied from other similar books. The main Mennonite source was a collection of 18 prayers by the well-known hymn writer Leenaerdt Clock, first published in 1625. It is particularly interesting to note in these prayers a recurring passage on behalf of those "good-hearted people who have shown genuine compassion to us through your grace" (p. 46). Known as half-Anabaptists, the prayers describe these people as having little strength to come into full obedience to God.

The prayers convey a vibrant belief in angels with such phrases as "And keep sending down to us your holy angels as loyal guides" or "Holy father, lead and direct me further on this journey through the protection of your dear angels" (p.79). One sees hints of the influence of Pietism.

Leonard Gross and Herald Press are to be commended for making this classic early Anabaptist work available to the English-speaking public. Until this English edition, most Mennonites have been virtually ignorant of the existence of any prayer book of Mennonite origin. I believe that spontaneous prayers should not be replaced with historic prayers, but our prayer heritage is hereby enriched. As the preface by the translator says, this is "One of the best-kept publishing secrets within the Anabaptist tradition" (p.11).

Gerald Studer is an historian and pastor who lives in Lansdale, Pennsylvania.

From Martyr to Muppy, edited by Alistair
Hamilton, Sjouke Voolstra and Piet Visser.
Amsterdam: Amsterdam University Press. 1994.

Reviewed by Gerlof D. Homan

Many students of Anabaptist-Mennonite history are
somewhat familiar with Dutch Mennonitism. They
know about the martyrs and the sixteenth century and
the Mennonites' cultural and economic achievements
and contributions to Dutch civilization in the seventeenth century. They have also studied their decline
and wonder if American Mennonites during their own
process of assimilation in the twentieth century might
not experience a similar fate. Unfortunately, relatively
few individuals have sufficient command of the Dutch
language to acquaint themselves with the vast amount
of Dutch Mennonite historical literature. This book will
help many in the English-speaking world learn about
various facets of Dutch Mennonitism not ordinarily
found in general history or other surveys.

From *Martyr to Muppy* is a collection of papers deliv-
ered at the Amsterdam Summer University between
August 31 and September 4, 1992 for the course,
"Mennonites in the Netherlands: From Martyr to
Muppy." Most of the presenters were Dutch, such as
Sjouke Voolstra, Piet Visser, and others. The only two
Americans were Mary Sprunger from Eastern
Mennonite University (Harrisonburg, Virginia) and
Andrew Fix from Lafayette College (Easton,
Pennsylvania). Edmund Kizik from the University of
Gdansk (Danzig, Poland) also participated.

The title might be a bit misleading because most of

the essays focus on the seventeenth century and say little about the period of the martyrs or the period after 1700. Nor do we find out what Dutch muppies are like today. Since space does not permit discussion of each of the 15 essays, a few comments on some of the papers must suffice.

Alistair Hamilton and Sjouke Voolstra provide the two introductory chapters. The former places Dutch Mennonitism in the larger context of European Anabaptism and sketches the development of the movement in the Netherlands and its characteristics. Voolstra adds further detail to Hamilton's comments and then focuses especially on some of the main splits and divisions among Dutch Mennonites. He concludes that Dutch Mennonitism gradually abolished the boundaries of the church without "spot or wrinkle" and became an a-confessional movement characterized by a "moderately rationalist, pietist and ethical faith." One is tempted to ask if American Mennonitism is awaiting the same fate.

Otto de Jong discusses the problem of Dutch Mennonitism and Dutch Protestantism. He traces Mennonite-Calvinist relations in the seventeenth century when Menno's followers were barely tolerated in the Dutch Republic. He concludes, however, with the interesting observation that today many Dutch Protestants have become more Mennonite since they confirm their members at a more advanced age. Kizik's paper on the Dutch Mennonites in the Vistula Delta and Gdansk is a good introduction to a very interesting story of Dutch Mennonite settlement in Eastern Europe. The essay contains new data but is a bit heavy on economic and legal history. One looks for more on cultural and religious developments. Many Mennonites across the Atlantic should be especially interested in the Dutch Mennonite experience in West Prussia because they are the descendants of these sixteenth-century refugees.

Very interesting are the two essays by Piet Visser. The first one discusses the negative, critical image of Mennonites in some sixteenth- and seventeenth-century Dutch literature. Just as the word "Dutch" often conveys a negative behavior or attitude in the English language, so the term "Mennonite" in Dutch sometimes came to mean something derogatory. Among such expressions were "Mennonite Lie," "Mennonite Wedding" and "Mennonite Trick." Interestingly, one of the most severe critics of the Mennonites was the author Pieter Langendijk (1683-1755), who was a Mennonite himself. The appendix of this article lists some 84 Dutch Mennonite authors and poets. This list might have been better placed at the end of Marijke Spies's essay on Mennonites and literature in the seventeenth century.

Visser's second essay discusses the fascinating Dutch businessman, minister, and writer Jan Philipsz Schabaelje (1592-1656), who became one of the most popular Mennonite authors of his time. Schabaelje's most important writing was *Lusthof des Gemoets* (Pleasure Garden of the Heart) which was translated into German and English as *Die wandlende Seele* and *The Wandering Soul*. Visser calls the *Lusthof des Gemoets* one of the "finest literary expressions of the Mennonite reform movement."

In the essay by Louis P. Grijp on Mennonite hymns and psalms in the sixteenth and seventeenth centuries we learn that many of the melodies were secular tunes.

However, because of a conservative melody choice by some poets, a number of originally secular melodies become the exclusive property of the Mennonites. These included many of the melodies of the so-called *Souterliedekens* or psalms. The prominent Dutch Mennonite Hans de Ries (1533-1638) included many of the latter in his well-known *Lietboeck* (Songbook) of which several editions appeared.

Mary Sprunger's fine contribution is a social and economic case study of the seventeenth-century Amsterdam Waterland Mennonite Church "Bij de Tooren" (Near the Tower), based primarily on Dutch Mennonite archival materials. The essay tells us much about the members' socio-economic status. For instance, we often assume that most seventeenth-century Dutch Mennonites were affluent. However, Sprunger points out that in this church some 15 to 18% of the members received poor relief from their congregation. Other members made substantial fortunes in trade, commerce, and industry. Many Waterland Mennonites were cloth merchants. Amsterdam Waterlanders were also influential in the Amsterdam Bank of Exchange in which at least 20 church board members held accounts in 1645. Especially interesting is Sprunger's discussion of the entrepreneur Arent Dircksz Bosch, a wealthy Waterland deacon, which shows how merchants made and invested capital. Yet, as Sprunger rightly concludes, although close family and social ties enabled the Waterland elite to amass sizable fortunes, Mennonites were not represented in the uppermost rung of Amsterdam's social and economic ladder.

While many Dutch Mennonites were busily engaged

in various prosperous economic activities, their theology was much affected by major seventeenth-century intellectual currents and controversies. Andrew Fix discusses the well-known story of the impact of rationalism, Collegiantism, Socinianism, Cartesianism, etc. He focuses especially on the so-called Lambs' War, which caused divisions in many Dutch Mennonite congregations. It is obvious that many facets of these events need much further study and research.

From Martyr to Muppy contains very little on the eighteenth century, a period during which Dutch Mennonites lost many members, most traditional beliefs, and their distinctive identity. Consequently, most were not at all reluctant to bear arms and gladly joined the revolution in 1795, which granted them the same rights as the Dutch Calvinist majority.

Voolstra briefly discusses the major events from 1795 to 1810, and then the period from 1810 to 1850, focusing especially on two leading Mennonite leaders and thinkers of that time, Samuel Muller and Douwe Simons Gorter. The former tried to recapture some Mennonite identity, while the latter concluded that it was impossible to preserve a distinct Christian community. In the end, Dutch Mennonites seemed to differ from many other Christians only in their refusal to take oaths and their belief in adult baptism. Voolstra challenges muppies to remember their martyred forebears who had no fear of being a distinct minority.

The final chapter by Anton van der Lem focuses principally on two leading twentieth-century historians of Mennonite descent, Johan Huizinga (1872-1945) and Jan Romein (1893-1962). One wonders if these two men deserved to be included. While both were baptized Mennonites, they were not active church members. Furthermore, it is not at all clear that their historical writings or their lifestyles reflected typically Mennonite values. When van der Lem contends that especially Romein's historical works showed his Mennonite background, he should have cited a few examples to prove his point.

The essays in *From Martyr to Muppy* are a very valuable contribution to Dutch Mennonite historiography and will undoubtedly stimulate much further discussion and research. They are all readable and smoothly translated, although one might disagree with some translations and stumble over a few spelling errors. Each essay also contains valuable bibliographical information. This volume is further graced by many interesting illustrations and four separate indexes.

Any student of Anabaptist-Mennonite history should read all or some of these essays. What befell Dutch Mennonites may very well happen to their brothers and sisters in the New World. Unfortunately, no essay tells us precisely and satisfactorily why Dutch Mennonites became what they are today. That subject deserves much further investigation and discussion.

Gerlof D. Homan writes from Normal, Illinois.

Film Ratings and Video Guide

Film Ratings and Video Guide 1995-1998

by Merle Good

The following capsule reviews rate movies which have shown in theaters (some are foreign films with very limited release) from an adult perspective on a scale from 1 (pathetic) through 9 (extraordinary), based on their sensitivity, artistry, integrity, and technique. These listings include a number of movies from the first half of 1998.

Absolute Power—An aging professional thief pulls off the ultimate jewel heist, only to witness a murder involving the President of the United States. Promising beginning sinks to melodrama. (2)

Addicted to Love—A silly movie with some good actors is still a silly movie. An awkward astronomer finds himself losing his girl to a French restaurant owner. So he spies on them. And the French guy's former girl joins the spy game. Right, silly it is. (3)

Afterglow—Julie Christie lights up the screen in this movie about middle age, unhappiness, and two tired marriages. The bored, unfulfilled spouses unknowingly find romance with the other's partner. Wears a bit thin. (5)

Air Force One—An action picture which stretches believability. The U.S. President battles terrorists on his own plane. (3)

The American President—The President is a liberal/centrist Democrat. He has a 12-year-old daughter. He also is a widower. This excellent film (directed by Rob Reiner) combines the fast pace of the White House with political tugs of war and a President dating a bright, beautiful lobbyist while his opponents criticize. Funny, thoughtful, and entertaining. (8)

Amistad—Based on the story of an actual revolt on a slave ship in 1839, this stilted but effective epic dramatizes the conflict between the slave owners and the abolitionists. Steven Speilberg errs on the side of making it a history lesson, but it's an excellent one for everyone. A must see. (7)

Anaconda—Ineffective. Set in the Brazilian rain forest, hunting down the monster, to shoot it (with both gun and camera). (2)

Apollo 13—A rare accomplishment. Director Ron Howard marshals the events of the flawed 1970 Apollo mission into a riveting adventure. The interplay of scientific precision with the humanity of the astronauts creates a marvelous texture and thrill. (9)

The Apostle—A stunning achievement by Robert Duvall who writes, directs, and stars in this masterful portrait of a failed religious man. Duvall neither mocks nor defends the charismatic Pentecostal preacher; he simply invites us to understand what it was like to be a mesmerizing preacher who, in spite of serious shortcomings, still hears the voice of God in his life. Courageous, artistic, and deeply moving. Few religious persons of the conservative or liberal persuasion could risk such an honest story of redemption and failure. (9)

As Good As It Gets—An excellently delivered film about the mellowing of a bigot. Problem is, to prove he's a bigot, he has to say some pretty offensive things. That aside, Jack Nicholson and Helen Hunt are top-notch. Sensitive in a bully sort of way. (8)

The Arrival—So-so yarn about an astronomer who picks up signals from intelligent life in space. (5)

Assassins—Above-average thriller about a high-tech hit man who's being undercut by a younger competitor just when he wants out. (4)

The Associate—A superb Wall Street broker can't rise to the top because of her race. So she starts her own company and invents a white partner for acceptability. Gets complicated. Not as funny or profound as it sounds. (4)

Babe—A delightful, surprisingly captivating story about a pig who wants to be a sheepdog. Adults may enjoy it even more than children. (8)

Bad Boys—A hip cop-buddy flick. Has some humor tucked away among the cliches as the twosome (surprise, surprise) case out a drug heist. (3)

Batman Forever—An intriguing designer-hued sequel to the successful cinematic spin-off of the TV series. A dark and gloomy struggle between Two-Face and his evil schemes and the reluctant Batman. (5)

Before the Rain—A highly original, poetic but involving portrait of conflict between Christians and Muslims in Macedonia. A young monk risks great danger by sheltering a young Muslim girl. Two other stories interweave. (8)

Before Sunrise—Low key, but charmingly engaging. A young American boy's meeting a French girl on a train becomes a rare encounter of soulmates. Funny and sweet. (6)

Beyond Rangoon—Picturesque adventure of a young American doctor on a sojourn to Burma, caught in the war in 1988. A bit boring and too heavy-handed—yet it's a beautiful trip. (4)

The Big Lebowski—There are few treats in the world of cinema to equal a new film by the Brothers Coen. While this is not their greatest of all time (*Raising Arizona, Fargo,* and *Barton Fink* are classics), *The Big Lebowski* has that same uncanny eye for human nature.

With the bowling alley lending stability to these bumbling characters, "the Dude" tries to figure out whether a millionaire's wife was or was not kidnapped. Ineptitude abounds with disaster an ever-present promise. Deliciously entertaining in its zany snapshots of life. (8)

The Big Night—A feast. A wonder, really. One of the best films in years. Two Italian immigrant brothers attempt to survive in the 1950s restaurant business. Conflict between artistry and commerce. Unfolds slowly— fast eaters should try a fast-food menu. But if the viewer wants to savor a great movie the way one settles back to relish a great book, this is the chef's special. (9)

Boogie Nights—Amateur trash to be avoided. Can't explain why Hollywood thought this low-grade non-story is avant-garde. (1)

Boys on the Side—A mixed-bag movie, overloaded with trendy themes (female bonding, men are bullies, AIDS, an unfulfilled lesbian). Three women on the road, but their wandering lacks focus. (4)

The Boxer—Daniel Day-Lewis shines as an IRA prisoner who returns to Belfast after 14 years in prison. He wants to go back to life, but many hurdles remain: a forbidden love, an unacknowledged betrayal, and a love of boxing. And of course, a politically charged atmosphere, soaked with centuries of hatred. Can he begin again? (7)

Brassed Off—-A small likeable picture about Yorkshire miners who keep their brass band going as an act of defiance after their coal pit is closed. (5)

Braveheart—An epic look at 13th-century Scottish leader William Wallace. Not a fine epic, mind you, but serviceable. Battle scenes outshine the human interest moments. (6)

Breakdown—A man and his wife from the big city, travelling through the American West, suffer a trauma approaching surrealism when their vehicle breaks down in the desert. His wife disappears, and everywhere

he turns for help, he can't tell if he's being mocked, conned, or if he's simply breaking down himself. Eerie and effective. (6)

Breaking the Waves—An unforgettable, unconventional film about a small unfriendly Scottish hamlet on the North Sea. A woman walks the edge, even as she struggles with fantasy, mystery, and conversations with God. Compellingly acted. (8)

The Bridges of Madison County—Somewhat solemn tale of a photographer who comes to Iowa to photograph covered bridges and falls in love with a local farmer's wife (who dreams way beyond the corn stalks). Has a stiff quality to a story that's supposed to be full of passion. Great acting. (6)

Broken Arrow—A fast-paced, constantly moving action-thriller about a disgruntled Air Force pilot (great performance by John Travolta) who kidnaps some nuclear weapons. Highly entertaining. (6)

The Brothers McMullen—Three Irish Catholic brothers from the suburbs of new York struggle to focus their lives after rough growing-up

273

days. Each of the three harbors mixed agenda about love, life, and faith. Oh—and there's a lot of talking. But worthwhile, nonetheless. (6)

Bulworth—This is either a profound political satire about impotence and hypocrisy—or it represents the most outrageous bigotry mainstreamed on the big screen in the name of farce. Or it might be a high-tempo study of a public person going over the edge. On the other hand, maybe Warren Beatty just wanted to do an offbeat comedy.

A senator up for re-election suddenly finds himself speaking the truth instead of politically correct nothings. Chaos arises on every side. Is it a gimmick or a tragedy? This viewer suspects clandestine political agenda stirring the waters of a wacky, unfocused farce. (5)

Burnt by the Sun—A lush, impressionistic look at a member of the secret police in the 1930s, set near the wheat fields outside Moscow. (6)

Bye Bye, Love—A step above sitcom, this mild comedy charts the aches and ironies of three regular guys, all divorced fathers, who struggle through a weekend of care and custody of their children. (6)

Career Girls—Two London college roommates meet after six years and compare notes and lives. Brisk dialogue and awkward situations populate the yearnings, memories, and sad sense of failure. But promise remains. (6)

Casino—Why can't Martin Scorscse have a sense of humor? This third quasi-epic about the mob is less engaging than his earlier, grittier films. But it so lacks humor. A look at a bookie, chosen by the mob to run a major casino in Las Vegas. A parable about Vegas is thrown in for free. Lacks personality, so the brutality seems without context. (4)

Circle of Friends—Three Catholic girls go off to school in 1950s Dublin. A warm-hearted love story, laced with some intrigue and betrayal. (6)

City of Angels—A dreamy yarn about an angel who escorts the dying into the next world. Only in hanging around the hospital, he falls in love with a doctor when he sees her crying after losing a patient. Deep meanings, presumably. Warm, engaging story nonetheless. (6)

City Hall—A crisis in the mayor's office as a tangled web unravels, enmeshed in political intrigue. A seasoned pro and a young idealist. (6)

Clerks—High energy, low quality, coarse-talking flick about some foul-mouthed guys who work at a convenience store in Jersey. Irritating coarseness overwhelms occasional humor. (2)

Clueless—A teen picture which wavers between cardboard stereotypes and would-be satire. A very rich Beverly Hills girl has more schemes for her friends' lives than for her own. (3)

Colonel Chabert—A gentle tragedy about a war hero who shows up in 1817 Paris, ten years after he has been declared dead. His wife has remarried and claimed his estate. Fine acting and superb storytelling. (7)

Con Air—Non-stop action picture about a man, unjustly imprisoned, who has his plane hijacked by convicts on his way home. A stroke above the average mindless boom-boom. (4)

Congo—Misfires. An interesting idea, which needs imaginative treatment, falls into the hands of formula filmmakers. A multinational corporation sets its sights on African treasures guarded by angry gorillas. (4)

Conspiracy Theory—A lot of racing around and worrying-for-nothing. A paranoid cab driver mixes reality and conspiracy theories and a justice department prosecutor tries to help out (he falls for her, of course). But it's flat. (4)

Contact—A radio astronomer picks up intelligent signals from outer space. Instructions are given on how to build the proper conveyance. But should the emissary to outer space believe in God? This engrossing story is one of the better ones. (7)

Cop Land—An above average yarn about a partly impaired cop becoming determined to take on those who underestimate him. Crime, corruption, and self-esteem in New Jersey (with New York across the river). (5)

Copycat—Hold on to your hat! This taut thriller teams an expert on serial killers with an intense, tough police investigator (Holly Hunter is great) as they try to outwit a serial killer who's hung up on history. (7)

Crimson Tide—As war movies go, with all of Hollywood's fine-tuning, this one is excellent. Two generations of military leaders clash over the meaning of war—bottled up in a nuclear sub at sea which loses its communication link. Very involving. Gene Hackman and Denzel Washington excel. (8)

The Crossing Guard— Father of a young girl who was killed in an accident obsessively plots his revenge. Uneven. (4)

Cry, the Beloved Country—A film masterpiece, based on a literary masterpiece set in South Africa in the 1940s. Touching portrait of two grieving fathers, etched against the backdrop of injustice. (8)

Dangerous Minds—A warmhearted story about an ex-Marine who puts her energy into being an inner-city schoolteacher. Not as gritty and hard-edged as one might expect, but worth your while. (7)

Dante's Peak—Avoid. Another disaster of a disaster picture—volcano this time. (1)

Daylight—OK, so they got me at the primal fear level in this disaster picture. A New York tunnel under the Hudson River collapses. Run! But it's a below average disaster picture, especially if you don't worry about tunnels the way I do. (2)

The Daytrippers—If you're ready to listen to other people talk and complain, this is for you. For solitude, make another selection. A family of suburbanites spends a harrowing day in New York, trying to learn the truth behind a mysterious love letter. Very funny if you don't mind the noise. (6)

Dead Man Walking—A masterfully directed and acted story of a Catholic nun who begins to visit a death row murderer. She's tougher than he thought. She also gets involved with the parents of the slain teenagers. Based on a true story. (9)

Desperate Measures—A good cop gets desperate when the only donor who matches his son's need for a bone marrow transplant is a psychopathic killer.

Desperate storyline leads to incredible measures. (2)

Devil in a Blue Dress—An excellent movie, set in black Los Angeles in 1948. A young man gets pulled into a web of intrigue and corruption, trying to keep his integrity and somehow survive. Superb drama about character in the middle of racism and the struggles of life in general. (9)

The Devil's Own—A less than satisfying yarn about an IRA terrorist who is inadvertently taken in by a straight-shooting New York cop. All mushed up. (3)

Dr. Dolittle—A smart-mouthed delight about a doctor who can talk with animals. Really. All the time. Could be a threat to job security. Not to mention family and good old sanity. Very funny some of the time, amusing the rest of the time. A bit raunchy for youngsters. (6)

Die Hard with a Vengeance—Relentless non-stop action film about a cop determined to outwit a bomber who's going to blow things up. Very effective as a grunting, breathless sequence of stunts. (4)

Deep Impact—A comet is going to destroy the earth. Maybe just parts of it. This formula disaster film has interesting moments and a number of outstanding performances, but the final result is of little impact. (3)

Disclosure—A slick, taut tease of a thriller. Brass knuckles in the work place. A hightech executive loses his promotion to an old girlfriend. It gets complicated as both accuse the other of sexual harassment. Frank but ambiguous. (5)

Dolores Claiborne—A riveting psychological thriller about a daughter who returns to her lonely Maine home to "visit" her mother, a crusty, tough woman accused of murder. Not as grisly as it sounds. Superb writing and acting. (7)

Don Juan de Marco—Sure, it's a fantasy of sorts, but it's clever and fun. Marlon Brando hands in a fine performance as a psychiatrist totally absorbed by the story of his young patient who is (or thinks he is) the legendary lover. Johnny Depp is superb. (7)

Donnie Brasco—A tender but violent film, brooding

over the thin line between loyalty and betrayal. A young FBI undercover agent begins to like the man he is set to trap. (6)

Down Periscope—An amusing light comedy about a hapless crew on an outdated submarine. (4)

The Edge—A hapless survival picture about a very rich man, his young beautiful wife, the young photographer who's having an affair with her, and the bear who would enjoy any lunch available. The bear's the best. (3)

The Englishman Who Went Up a Hill But Came Down a Mountain—A mildly amusing yarn about a Welsh town who has their mountain measured, only to discover it's a hill—and the solutions they pursue. (5)

Eve's Bayou—A masterfully realized gem, painful and unforgettable. A young black girl in Louisiana remembers her family, with all of the boisterousness, broken relationships, secrets, and binding ties. Tender, exquisite, and moving. (8)

Evita—You'll probably either like it a lot—or not like it a lot. A musical film—no spo-

ken words—lifted by an excellent performance by Madonna as Eva Peron, from poverty to First Lady of Argentina (1940s). Mesmerizing music. (7)

Executive Decision—A thriller about a military team who boards a hijacked jet loaded with a bomb and tear gas. (4)

Face/Off—A spectacular film about the good guy and the bad guy trading faces. Riveting. So who's hunting whom—the F.B.I. man or the assassin? Nicholas Cage and John Travolta are tops. Only weakness emerges from the gimmicks going overboard. (7)

Fargo—An inventive murder tale which swings between the grisly and the humorous, assembled by the Brothers Coen. Based on a true story. A botched kidnapping gets complicated. Not for queasy stomachs. Study of pregnant sheriff worth the ticket. (8)

Fierce Creatures—Fierce disappointment. Those who enjoyed *A Fish Called Wanda* will despair at this misfire by the same cast. A business man decides a zoo should be run to make profits. (2)

The Fifth Element—A lark. Bruce Willis as a 23rd-century cab driver. Visually dazzling and imaginative as he teams up with a beautiful alien (of course) to save the world from the evil forces which are unleashed every 5,000 years. (6)

First Knight—Why does Richard Gere ruin every picture he's in? Because he can't bring himself to play anyone beside pretty boy Richard Gere, I guess. A fresh spin on the Camelot story turns to mush fit to flush. A pity. (3)

Flirting with Disaster—An off-the-wall comedy about a young man who can't name his son until he finds his real parents (he was adopted). Fast-paced. (5)

Fools Rush In—Energetic cross-cultural romance which runs out of steam. Fast-climbing New York company guy falls for tough Las Vegas photographer. They rise to the challenge, determined that love will prevail. (5)

Forget Paris—An NBA referee meets an airline agent in Paris. They fall in love. But how to live? Sometimes funny, sometimes disappointing. (5)

French Kiss—A B-grade, paint-by-the-numbers yarn about a young woman who's been jilted and tries to get him back or get even. (3)

A Friend of the Deceased—A black comedy about the black market in the new Ukraine, reflecting on the break-up of the Soviet Union. Greed, mobsters, and unemployed intellectuals. (4)

The Full Monty—A bawdy British comedy about a group of unemployed steelworkers who decide to form a male strip troupe as a way of making some money. Poignant, political, and funny by spells. (4)

G. I. Jane—This movie tries to have it both ways and fails. Demi Moore plays the first woman candidate for Navy SEAL training. But clearly the camera wants us to see Demi Moore's body more than tell a story. Strong action sequences. (4)

The Game—A control-freak business tycoon has his life spun out of control by a gift from his less-than-successful brother. A wild adventure ensues, playing on the paranoid fears of the tycoon. But in the end, neither is as cheated as the audience is. Kerrr-plunk. (4)

Gattica—A thoughtful science fiction thriller about a future world separated into perfect lab babies and human babies (not perfect). Too heavy for action seekers; too manipulated to be profound. (5)

Get Shorty—Some films are delicious. What would happen, for instance, if a mobster went to Hollywood? Who would outwit whom? Throw in John Travolta and Danny De Vito, and you've got a tasty yarn. A delicious, well-written, well-acted, well-directed con job. (7)

Ghosts of Mississippi—Assistant D.A. reopens case against the killer of civil rights leader Medgar Evers. Seems too much like a showcase for mediocre Alec Baldwin. But worthwhile nonetheless. (5)

The Glass Shield—A cut above the average cop picture, highlighting prejudice and miscarriage of justice in the police department in L.A. (4)

Go Now—Poignant story of an energetic day laborer who loves to play soccer. His life is upended when he discovers that he has multiple sclerosis. Tender portrait of friendship. (6)

Golden Eye—This latest James Bond movie stars Pierce Brosman, charming but somewhat spineless. The genre mainly depends on gadgets, sight gags, and beautiful women (some of whom want to kill Bond). As such, it delivers its light entertainment. But nothing more. (4)

Good Will Hunting—In a class of its own, this rare film excels in every way—writing, acting, directing, nuance, storyline, paradox. A working class janitor can solve M.I.T.'s most difficult problems (as he mops up their hallway), but he doesn't want to give up his neighborhood and his crude but loyal friends.

Enter a beautiful Harvard student and the tension builds. What should a genius do to find peace? Matt Damon is extraordinary as Will Hunting. Robin Williams tries to help as a failed but wiser shrink. And the poor rich girl—how can she compete?

This movie holds it all together, with energy and wit burning up the edges. Unforgettable. (9)

Gone Fishin'—Two fishermen go adventuring in Florida and run into trouble. Booooring. (1)

Great Expectations—Parables are hard to stretch for two hours. Improving upon Charles Dickens makes it even more difficult. Turns out this yarn about the rise of a poor artist and the rich girl who keeps re-appearing fails. (3)

Grosse Pointe Blank—Perhaps the funniest hour of black comedy ever filmed (apart from the Coen Brothers)—that's how superb the first half of this movie is. A hit man goes home for his 10-year class reunion. His old flame is a local radio disc jockey. But it's so rare that a funny first half is followed by a funny second half. Here the movie moves from hip to rip. A mistake. Nonetheless, the first half is incredibly funny. (6)

Grumpier Old Men—Amiable yarn about two foul-mouthed but harmless old men. Waste of talent. (3)

Hackers—Several young computer whiz kids take on a corporate bad guy who's trying to frame them. Has its moments. (4)

Hamlet—The first full-length film version of the Shakespeare classic. A visual feast as we empathize with the very human characters in this tale of intrigue, suspicion, betrayal, and tragedy. A towering accomplishment. (8)

He Got Game—A hard-art look at the father-son relationship in the black American experience. Spike Lee mixes poetry with grit in this tale set in the world of modern basketball—dreams of money, realities of poverty, and deception. Well done. (7)

Heat—A rigorous tug-of-war between a hardnosed thief and a tenacious cop, elegantly etched and spun, yet a bit much. (5)

Heavenly Creatures—A highly imaginative re-creation of a true-life sensational murder in new Zealand in the '50s. Artful dissection of the vivid fantasies, intense friendship, and murderous attitudes of the two girls. (6)

Hideaway—A man is brought back to life after having been dead too long. A mediocre science-fiction thriller about a psychic connection to a killer. (3)

WHAT MENNONITES ARE THINKING, 1998

Home for the Holidays—
Family gathering as trauma.
Worthwhile bittersweet
depiction of a fractured
family who gathers for
Thanksgiving. Funny, sad,
and even somewhat hopeful.
(7)

Hoodlum—A disappointing
attempt to portray the real-
life godfather of Harlem in
the '30s, Ellsworth "Bumpy"
Johnson. Great photography
does not a drama make. (4)

Hope Floats—Uneven story
about a woman who learns—
on a live TV show—that her
husband is having an affair
with her best friend. She
moves home and seeks roots,
stability, and contentment
with her young daughter and
her eccentric mother. (5)

The Horse Whisperer—A
charmingly patient picture
about a broken horse, a broken girl, an impatient
woman, and a mysterious
man from the lush Montana
skyscapes. Whether Robert
Redford (as director) is being
condescending—or simply
patient—remains a puzzle.
Perhaps we'll never know
until we crouch in the tall
Montana grass and wait. (7)

**How to Make an American
Quilt—**A major disappointment. Lacks focus, depth,
story, and soul. A graduate
student spends a summer
with her grandmother and
her quilting group. (5)

The Hunted—C-grade yarn
about an American businessman in Japan who gets
caught in ferocious ninja
crossfire. (1)

Hush— A mediocre melodrama about a young wife
who has to battle her mother-in-law for the loyalties of
"Mama's boy." Turns out
Mama has secrets of her
own. (2)

The Ice Storm—Plays like a
filmed play, all in winter, of
course. And the actors are as
reluctant as the characters
they play. Two families
unravel as the father from
one sleeps with the mother
from the other. Never quite
gets past the dress rehearsal,
though it has its moments. (4)

I Like It Like That—A moving portrait of a Latino
woman, caught in poverty, a
troubled marriage, and Bronx
noise. Vibrant tone tran-
scends usual cliches. (7)

Immortal Beloved—A
flawed but partly successful
attempt to look into the
mind of the great composer

Beethoven. Wild-goose-chase to locate his mystery lover seems like a side street, but there are unforgettable moments. (5)

In and Out—Nothing is so tedious as a pretentious vehicle which announces itself to be a pioneering, courageous breakthrough. A thoroughly boring film about a student who thanks his teacher (on national television) and then announces that the teacher is gay. (2)

In Love and War—- Unfortunate film based on Ernest Hemingway's WWI love affair with a Red Cross nurse. The pieces don't add up to a whole. (4)

The Indian in the Cupboard—A warm, engaging fantasy about a 9-year-old boy and the plastic Indian in his cupboard which comes alive. (6)

I.Q.—Stilted but funny story about several retired scientific geniuses (including Einstein played by Walter Matthau) who experiment at maneuvering such unscientific things as romance. Quite charming. (6)

The Jackal—A below-average international hit-man/ter-rorist picture, complete with multiple disguises. (2)

Jackie Brown—A rather engaging film about a smart (and beautiful) flight attendant who tries to outrun both the gun smuggler and the government agent. Best performance by the gentle parole officer (Robert Forster) who tries not to fall for her. (7)

Jade—A dark, manipulative, and manipulated action film about scandal and sex in high places. (2)

Jefferson in Paris—Forget it. Even if you love history and costume pictures, forget it. An un-story about Thomas Jefferson, though it's hard to tell. (2)

Jerry Maquire—A rip-snort delight. A super-successful sports agent has an encounter with conscience—takes a tumble, notices a woman, bonds with her (very funny) son—and tries to get up again. Superb acting and writing overcomes any weaknesses in believability. Some unforgettable scenes. (7)

Johnny Mnemonic—A boring futuristic flick about a "wet-wired brain" who

283

absorbs huge amounts of data, pursued by gangsters. (1)

Judge Dredd—Set in futuristic Mega-City One, based on a comic strip. A total failure. (1)

Just Cause—Watch out. This film begins innocently enough as a story about capital punishment and the miscarriage of justice. But it becomes a high-voltage thriller. Fine acting by Sean Connery and Lawrence Fishburne. (6)

Kolya—A touching Czech film about a man who is completely broke, marries for money, loses his bride, and inherits a five-year-old boy. Tender and beautiful. (6)

Kiss of Death—A gritty, over-wrought film about a man caught between the law and the mob. Simply doesn't jell. (3)

Kiss the Girls—An unsettling picture about violence against women by a stalker/killer. Mediocre story slips into sadist exploitation. (2)

L' America—An uneven tale of two Italian businessmen, trying to cash in on the situation in post-Communist Albania. (4)

L.A. Confidential—An engaging *film noir*, set in the shadows of 1953 Los Angeles. A mobster goes to jail and the cops covet the turf. Ambition, integrity and the lack thereof, and the allure of money, sex, and power slip among the smart shades, complex nuances, and violent outbursts of finely-drawn characters. (9)

Ladybird, Ladybird—An empathetic study of the breakdown of the British welfare system. The mother is not without fault, but the system keeps taking her children away from her. Hard to forget. (7)

The Last Good Time—Half class, half exploitation. Engaging, poignant portrait of an aging widower who loves his memories and his violin. His relationship with a young girl requires implausible leaps. (4)

The Last Seduction—A sensuous, gritty thriller about a clever woman who lays traps for men. This tramp is good, but her lying is running up a tab. Fast paced and witty. (6)

Last Summer in the Hamptons—Perhaps it was meant to be a satire about three generations of a family of actors. Maybe not. Whatever, it's flat. (2)

Leaving Las Vegas—An engaging study of a depressing subject. A man determined to drink himself to death goes to Las Vegas and meets a sympathetic hooker. Classic portrait of two losers. (9)

Legends of the Fall— Would-be saga set in the Montana Rockies in the early 20th century. Three brothers and their widowed father fight each other and court the beautiful woman who arrives from Boston. Too stagey for belief, but visually inviting. (4)

Les Miserables—A serviceable rendition of a classic story of misery, the hunter and the hunted, the burden of forgiveness, the burden of the law, and true love in 19th century France. A police officer is determined, after many years, to arrest a thief who seems similar to the man who is now mayor. Highly recommended, even though it's a bit slow. (7)

Liar, Liar—An amusing fantasy about a lawyer who can't tell a lie. If you can make the leap of faith. (4)

Little Odessa—Low-key pace and strong performances combine in this small film about a hit-man from a Russian émigré neighborhood who returns home against the wishes of everyone but his younger brother. (5)

Little Women—A first-rate classic. Wonderful masterpiece about four New England daughters and their mother surviving hard times. Based on Louisa May Alcott's classic novel. (9)

Looking for Richard—A truly imaginative gem. Worth seeing more than once. Al Pacino directs and stars in this delightful film about the performing of Shakespeare's *Richard III.* (8)

Losing Isaiah—A heart tugger. A black crack mom abandons her baby in a garbage can. A caring white social worker adopts the baby. But the biological mother repents, goes clean— and wants her Isaiah back. Well acted. (7)

The Lost World: Jurassic Park—OK, so we got those special effects dinosaurs again. What's the point? No madness and chaos this time, just lots of special effects. (4)

Mad City—A manipulative film about a TV reporter who tries to manipulate a small crisis into a major showdown, all for the commercial interest of ratings. Old news. (3)

The Madness of King George—A delicious treat about leadership and madness. This historical re-creation of the life of the king who lost the American colonies juxtaposes a witty, ebullient king with a dowdy, declining monarch. Brilliant acting. Crisp poetry. (8)

The Man in the Iron Mask—This swashbuckler's action buckles more than it swashes. Ho-hum tale of a French king who keeps his twin brother imprisoned until the Musketeers try to free him. Not quite convincing. (4)

The Man Who Knew Too Little—Granted, the title's the best part. An American in London, caught between make-believe and reality. (2)

Marius and Jeannette—A delightfully delineated portrait of the romantic relationship between a cement factory guard and a strong-willed supermarket cashier. In French. (7)

Marvin's Room—A deeply moving look at family ties—or the strain of old wounds. Excellent acting and direction. A woman who has devoted her adult life to taking care of her father who's disabled by a stroke, as well as an eccentric aunt—this woman now needs to reach out to her estranged sister for help because of a problem she faces. Sensitive and fine. (8)

Mary Reilly—A totally slow, unsatisfying Jekyll-and-Hyde yarn. Dumb. (1)

Men in Black—Tommy Lee Jones and Will Smith loom larger than life in this rump of science-fiction, action, wise-cracking surrealism. More than a thousand aliens are residing on earth secretly, many for their own protection. The movie's great fun, almost serious at times, but mainly a superb entertainment. (7)

Mercury Rising—A flawed FBI agent tries to protect an autistic child from hit men. Has a bit of heart, but it's mainly a Bruce Willis action flick. (2)

Metro—Average action picture about a hostage negotiator, unpredictable clutter, and a runaway cable car. (2)

Michael—An old woman's claim that an angel is living with her turns out to be true. Only the angel has his own persona. Very funny at points, charming, and a bit of a stretch. (6)

Microcosmos—A highly recommended documentary which studies the miniature living creatures (insects). Astonishing photography. Truly delightful (though it doesn't sound like it!). (9)

Midnight in the Garden of Good and Evil—An eccentric antique dealer stands trial for murder in murky, moody Savannah. Nasty, arrogant, languid, semi-opaque. A journalist seeks for the truth where only shadows of the mind roar and whisper. (5)

Milk Money—Wasted energy. An innocent enough yarn about a 12-year-old boy who tries to find a mate for his widowed dad and inadvertently chooses a kind hooker. (1)

Mission Impossible—Spin-off movie from ideas and characters of old TV show. Seems like spruced-up TV. Undercover agent in Prague. (4)

Mr. Holland's Opus—A wonderful, warmhearted story, spanning the 30-year career of a high school music teacher who wants to be a composer. Sentimental and a bit manipulative, but very worthwhile. (8)

Mrs. Brown—Sometimes a film tries very little and, within that restricted framework, accomplishes a great deal. That's the case here. A slowly engaging story of the relationship between grief-stricken Queen Victoria and the Highlands Scot groom whose audacity sparks her back to life. The performance of Billy Connolly as John Brown is one of the best of the year. (8)

Mrs. Dalloway—Set in 1923 London, based on a novel by Virginia Woolf. By all appearances, a candidate for "Masterpiece Theater," were it not for the magnificent performance of Vanessa Redgrave as Clarissa Dalloway, ever so proper on the surface, but brooding underneath about whether she married the wrong man. (6)

Money Talks—A fast-talking, nonstop motormouth involves a TV newsman in trying to prove he's not a bigger con than he is. Save your money. (2)

Money Train—Two cops (also foster brothers, one white and one black) confront the problems of the transit system in New York City. Funny, romantic, and suspenseful look at their relationship, but the movie's flaws hamper the effort. (5)

Mother—Small, charming comedy about a twice-divorced man who moves back to his mother to try to think through the root of his problems. Gently entertaining. (5)

Mulholland Falls—A cliché-endowed wannabe about police corruption in murky L.A. Mediocre. (2)

Murder at 1600—Lackluster adventure, tracking down the killer who snuffed out a woman at a well-known address. (2)

Muriel's Wedding—An offbeat Australian comedy about a young woman from a definitely dysfunctional family who hopes to get married by trying on wedding dresses. Funny and poignant by spells. (6)

My Best Friend's Wedding—An endearing tale about a writer who doesn't know how much she loves her old boyfriend until he announces he's marrying another woman. She promptly rushes to Chicago to break up the wedding with one low trick after another. Picture works in spite of thin characterizations. (6)

Nell—A highly engaging story about a "wild child" from Appalachian isolation who's never encountered modern civilization. Visually stunning. Two doctors disagree about how to treat Nell after her mother dies. (7)

Never Talk to Strangers—A thriller about a criminal psychologist who's being stalked by someone she knows—but whom? Has a contrived tone to the whole picture. So-so. (4)

The Net—A lot of fun, mainly because of an outstanding performance by Sandra Bullock. She plays a stubborn, very bright computer whiz who uncovers a top-secret scam to destabilize public life. (7)

Nick of Time—An accountant's daughter is kidnapped by terrorists and will be killed at 1:30 p.m. today—

unless the accountant assassinates the governor before 1:30 p.m. today. Full of suspenseful moments, but somehow comes off gimmicky. (5)

Night Falls on Manhattan—An overwrought Sidney Lumet film about New York, loud vulgarity, compromised police, and district attorneys who parade ambition in the guise of public honor. (5)

Nine Months—A lark. Hey, it's not perfect, but it captures many of the feelings of a woman and a man when they're expecting or not expecting a baby. Charming and funny. (7)

Nixon—Oliver Stone manipulates whatever he touches. Yet he spares Richard Nixon in many ways. An involving look at the moody president. (6)

Nobody's Fool—A nearly perfect "small picture." Paul Newman's finely tuned, subtle rendition of Sully, a small-town, broken-down contractor who's mostly out of work, is marvelous to watch. Sully's long-estranged son returns with Sully's grandson, and responsibility beckons the great avoider. Deeply emotive slice of life. Excellent. (9)

Nothing to Lose—A delightful picture after a really bad, no-good day. Tim Robbins plays Nick Beam, a super-successful ad exec whose world comes crashing down when he finds his wife in bed with his boss. He decides he has nothing to lose. Hilarious comedy. (6)

The Nutty Professor—A crude comedy designed as a showcase for Eddie Murphy which merely shows there's a case to be made for some pictures not to be made. (1)

One Fine Day—Lightweight but pleasant enough. Two harried parents meet in the middle of their hectic schedules and find some comfort in each other's troubles and presence. (5)

187—Well-intentioned picture about a teacher who is stabbed by an upset student. The teacher won't give up. (4)

Othello—A brilliant adaptation of the great Shakespearean tragedy. Superb acting and directing. A story of love, sabotaged by intrigue, jealousy, and evil. (9)

Out to Sea—This time Walter Matthau and Jack Lemmon flop. Intended comedy about two old guys on a cruise ship full of wealthy women. (3)

Out of Sight—An above-average caper film involving a bank robber who makes contact (literally) with a female federal marshall during a jail break. Will she take him in or be taken in by him? Or is she simply a step ahead? Entertaining. (6)

Outbreak—Hang on to your hat! Dustin Hoffman plays the military scientist in this fast-paced action film about a virus which can wipe out the entire U.S. population in several days. Very much fun. (7)

Paradise Road—A deeply moving story of a group of women who are taken prisoners during World War II. They fight to keep their sanity in the Japanese POW camp by forming a choir and performing classical music. Small, poignant story. (7)

The Peacemaker—Ho-hum international espionage flick with lots of action and little character. Agents try to outsmart terrorists who want to nuke Manhattan to call attention to Bosnia. (4)

A Perfect Murder—Perfect can be so perfect that it gets

boring. Somehow the jeopardy is lost in this mechanical Hollywoodish murder mystery. Waste of talent. (4)

Persuasion—An excellent portrayal of Jane Austen's story of a young woman who is taken for granted by her selfish family and by others. Has a Cinderella ending. (9)

Picture Perfect—A B-grade flick about an ad executive who makes up a fiance so she can make the man in the office jealous. (2)

Ponette—An exquisite film devoted to the point of view of a 4-year-old girl who loses her mother in an automobile accident. Later abandoned by her father, Ponette is forced to cope in a new setting, with an aunt. A portrait at once heartbreaking and wonderful. Excellent acting and directing. (8)

The Portrait of a Lady—Confusing tale of an independent American woman who goes to Europe and passes up marriage to an English lord for an unhappy life with a mean and irresponsible man. (3)

The Postman—A gentle gem. An Italian movie about a quiet peasant who discovers conversation, life, and love when a visiting poet takes time for him. (8)

The Preacher's Wife—It feels as though the producers wanted to produce a Christmas picture with an African-American setting which will run on TV for several generations. Good idea. The problem—the story lacks energy and credibility. But it'll probably still run on TV. An angel is sent down to help a struggling clergyman, but he (the angel) can't keep his eyes (etc.) off the preacher's wife. (5)

Queen Margot—A lavish costume drama set in 16th century France. Epic saga of war, greed, lust, and betrayal (and love?)—in the struggle between the Catholics and the Huguenots. Passionate magnificence seldom seen in films anymore. (7)

The Quick and the Dead—An old-style western with the modern twist of the mystery gunshooter in town being a woman with an unknown past. Has its moments. (4)

The Rainmaker—Francis Ford Coppola delivers a sharp-edged tale of a young lawyer, struggling against great odds. Engaging and funny. Not a masterpiece, but a worthwhile entertainment. (6)

Ready to Wear—Robert Altman brings his quick cuts and ironic critique to Paris and the fashion industry's shallow exploitation. Only this time it's a bore, perhaps because he fails to find his discipline and metaphor. Passing fad. (3)

Red—An intricate, scrumptious puzzle of a movie which ends up tasting more like a smorgasbord than a feast. Very entertaining tale about the oblique relationship between a young woman and an old retired judge who meet by accident. (7)

Red Corner—First of all, Richard Gere can't act. Secondly, the plot is overheated. Third, the ending makes no sense. Otherwise brilliant. An American entertainment lawyer (let us pause together to all shed a tear!) is imprisoned in China, accused falsely of murder. (2)

Restoration—A sumptuous film about a London doctor in the 1600s who is caught between service and pleasure. Melodramatic and unfocused. (4)

WHAT MENNONITES ARE THINKING, 1998

Richard III—A superb modern adaptation of Shakespeare's great play about villainy, set in an imagined fascist England of the 1930s. A brilliant film about tyranny. (9)

Rob Roy—Even the best of actors can't save this history epic. The story of Robert Roy MacGregor, 18th century Scottish legend, has its moments. But in the end it has no center, no heart. (4)

The Rock—High-octane action thriller about a Marine general who holds Alcatraz and threatens to detonate San Francisco. (4)

Romeo and Juliet—A daringly stylized, modern adaptation of the classic Shakespearean tragedy of lovers from rival clans being destroyed by the old hatreds from their families. Very engaging, visually stunning, daring use of color and juxtapositions. A superb achievement. And fun to boot. (9)

Romy and Michele's High School Reunion—A light comedy which will connect with all who've gone back to their class reunions. Two young women prepare to impress all their classmates,

but encounter major hurdles (sorta like high school itself). (6)

Sabrina—An old-fashioned romance about a chauffeur's daughter who dreams of catching the attention of the sons of her father's employer. (7)

The Saint—A James Bond type, with an attempt at deeper moorings. Doesn't quite work. An international thief sets about to steal the secret of free energy, but finds romance complicating things. (4)

The Scarlett Letter—It's not a classic, and it's only loosely based on Hawthorne's classic. But this film about forbidden love in an austere society has its moments. (6)

Secrets and Lies—A truly excellent film. A young black woman goes looking for her birth parents in a working-class neighborhood (in England). Surprises and hurts, secrets and lies, hope and small moments of grace. Slow paced—but if you gear down and let it absorb you, it's one of the best. (9)

The Secret of Roan Irish—A fantasy-legend-story about a young girl who listens to her grandparents' ancient magical tales by the Irish seaside. Beautiful, mystical, and involving. (6)

Sense and Sensibility—A mannered but highly engaging film about two sisters without a dowry, the shame, the anguish, and the love they feel. Set in Jane Austen's 1800s England. Superbly fine-tuned. (9)

Set It Off—A misfire. Four black women from L.A. poverty decide to take things into their own hands and rob banks. But the director can't decide if it's comedy, social commentary, or a hard-edged urban action flick. Disappointing. (3)

Seven—An intense but brutal mystery, shockingly and poetically etched against urban decay. A clever killer torments the police by punishing the seven deadly sins. (5)

Shall We Dance?—A superb story, set in Japan, about the secret passion of ballroom dancing. A shy accountant is drawn by a face he sees from a train—and step by step, his life changes. Careful balance, exquisite restraint, and excellent acting and directing. A metaphor, surely. (9)

The Shawshank Redemption—A splendidly acted masterpiece about two men in jail for life and the freedom they discover which eluded them before they came. (8)

Shine—A film that grabs you and won't let you go. A creative young pianist experiences emotional breakdown under the relentless, suffocating watch of his father. Years of dysfunction are capped with a return to music. Bravo performance by Geoffrey Rush. Wonderful music. (9)

Sliding Doors—Some ideas are more interesting than the execution. Here's an example. What if a British career girl catches the subway train and learns the truth about her boyfriend? On the other hand, what if she misses the train? The film unfolds as two interwoven lives. But the doubleknit doesn't fit. (3)

Sling Blade—A remarkable etching of a tale about a mentally deficient man. He tries to re-enter the real world after 20 years in prison for killing his mother when he was a child. He misunderstood then, and he struggles to understand now.

A marvelous performance by Billy Bob Thornton. (9)

Something to Talk About— A struggle between father and daughter, set in horse country. At times witty, at times a bit shallow. Decent acting by Julia Roberts and Robert Duvall. (5)

The Spanish Prisoner— When David Mamet is involved, you know the art form will be stilted and stylized. Half the time it ends up as pretentious hash. But the other half is some of the best around.

This movie is one of the better. Keep your eyes on the screen and listen carefully to Mamet's clipped conversations. Sly and engaging, a young inventor seems overwhelmed by the rich and powerful. He doesn't trust anyone, yet he must. A psychological thriller about con artists and shadowy fear. (9)

Species—A sci-fi-horror-exploitation film about a tentacled creature who takes the form of a beautiful young girl in order to mate. Save your money. (1)

Speechless—Two speech writers from opposing political campaigns fall for each other. The movie falls flat. (3)

Speed 2: Cruise Control— This sequel doesn't begin to match the fun of the first. A cruise ship gets hijacked by a mad computer expert. (3)

Sphere—A waste of good actors. Scientists discover a spacecraft on the bottom of the ocean—and they go to explore. So-so. (3)

Steal Big, Steal Little—It's like a big Latino family squabble, see. And the same actor plays both brothers. At moments it pretends to be a poignant classic, but it's mainly a jumbled mess about a rich family battling over an estate. (5)

Strange Days—A highly provocative film which blurs real experience with high-tech voyeurism of other persons' experiences, including sex and murder. Set in the not-too-distant future, a peddler of vicarious thrills has his game boomerang. Stylishly manipulative. (6)

Surviving Picasso—A thin ditty about the famous artist and his abusive relationship with women. A new woman decides she's different and tries to cultivate a relationship with Picasso. (4)

Tin Cup—Should one go for it—or should you pull up? A

marvelous story of a golf pro has-been who tries to win his rival's girlfriend and the big game in the same swing. But should he? (8)

Titanic—OK, so the young teenage girls got carried away and bought multiple tickets, making this the most popular film in history. The fact remains—this film deserves an audience because it is ingeniously made. Consider the facts. Not only does the audience know what's going to happen before they enter the theater. (The Titanic, in real life, sank into the ocean, in case you hadn't heard.) But the film opens with a story within a story, detailing exactly how the ship went down (with computer graphics showing every detail).

It takes a storyteller to hold an audience if they already know the ending. It takes a superb storyteller to so capture the telling that the audience weeps. That, in a nutshell, is what this film accomplishes.

Is it the greatest film ever made? No. Much of the acting is merely above average. It's the sense of jeopardy, the knowledge that some will survive and others won't, the incredible photography of the bodies in the cold

water—it's the marshaling of the story that triumphs here. The fictional young couple, from different classes of life, adds great emotional continuity. But this one belongs to James Cameron as writer and director. He avoids disaster movie clichés and creates a suspense where most directors can't find any. (8)

That Thing You Do—A labor of love by Tom Hanks (he also wrote the script and some of the songs) about the improbable rise to stardom of a no-name band from Erie, Pa. Set in 1964, it has a charm and innocence that makes it likeable. (6)

To Die For—A tragedy. With Nicole Kidman in the lead role, this could have been a classic comedy-tragedy. But it never leaves the station. A small-time reporter plots her way to the big time. (3)

To Live—A very involving Chinese film, following a couple and their family from the '40s to the '70s, with all of the cultural and political changes. A warm but startling story. (7)

Tom and Viv—A dark, brooding portrait of T.S. Eliot and his difficult relationship with his first wife. Under-stated, at times almost stony, and yet poetically knitted. (6)

Tommy Boy—A buffoon of a movie. An overwrought comedy about a not-so-bright son who suddenly must save the family business. (2)

Tomorrow Never Dies—A lightweight outing for James Bond (played by Pierce Brosman this time). A media mogul tries to start a war and James is called to the rescue. Bond flicks are not expected to be profound, but even the visuals seem tired. (2)

Toy Story—The first, full-length, completely computer-generated, animated movie. Ever. If that doesn't impress you, you may still enjoy this story of toys who come to life and are full of compassion, compared to that bad boy next door. Adults may enjoy it as much as kids. (7)

Trial and Error—A half-baked comedy about an actor who tries to impersonate a lawyer. (2)

The Truman Show—Probably a classic for years to come. Has technology virtually changed our lives so much that no one knows what and who is real? Must a society

that turns on money sacrifice the reality of human lives? Is there no morality left except television ratings? If one steps through that open doorway, will the life on the other side have less pretense and manipulation?

Peter Weir artfully directs what seems like the saga of an average Joe, Truman Burbank (sic), who begins to discover that his ordinary life is actually the longest running show in television history. May be worth seeing twice. Ed Harris excels as the show's creator/manipulator. (8)

The Truth about Cats and Dogs—Contains one of the funniest scenes ever filmed. A guy with a dog falls in love with a pet therapist/radio talk host without having met her. Self-conscious about her appearance, she gets her dumb but beautiful friend to meet him, impersonating her. A lark. (7)

Twilight—The actors are great fun to watch, even though the plot's messed up and the writing's weak. A has-been detective stumbles into a web involving his employer in this '40s neo-*noir*. (5)

Twister—A dramatic thriller tracing a group of tornado

chasers who get as close as they can to the destructive funnels so they can better understand them. Story lumbers, but effects are sizzling. (5)

Ulee's Gold—Peter Fonda's stellar performance as an inexpressive beekeeper in the Florida panhandle. His wife has died, his son's in jail, his daughter-in-law's in trouble, and he's trying to raise the grandchildren. It's all bottled inside, ready to blow up. A patient portrait of a man overwhelmed by life and his broken family. (7)

Up Close and Personal— An ambitious weathergirl fights her way to the top of the ladder of TV news, aided by a seasoned pro who seems on his way down. Has some strong moments. Engaging. (7)

The Usual Suspects—A delicious mystery drama, slowly unfolding, full of smoke and mirrors. Five professional thieves, a shipload of cocaine, and a determined interrogator. (7)

Volcano—Really lousy disaster movie. Volcano in L.A. (1)

Wag the Dog—OK, so we know there's a political sub-text. If we can swallow that part and accept the premise that Presidents begin wars to divert attention from their own personal scandals, then we've got an entertainment here. Otherwise the implausibility undercuts the whole story.

A make-believe war is staged on TV news to shape the opinion of a gullible, watching world. (5)

Waiting to Exhale—The story is weak but the acting is strong. Four women muse on life, love, and disappointment. (6)

A Walk in the Clouds—By the director of *Like Water for Chocolate,* this passionate fantasy about two young people who pretend to be married for the protection of the young woman from her father—leads to love, conflict, and fire (of course). (6)

Waterworld—Forget all the press about this big budget picture. As a land-less adventure on the edge of civilization in the future, this film delivers thrills, surprises, and moments you've never anticipated. (6)

The Wedding Singer—A good-natured, affectionate study of an unlikely subject.

Low-key portrayal of a failed rock singer who now sings at weddings and other affairs. All around nice guy, really. But is romance a possibility for those who sing at weddings? (6)

While You Were Sleeping— A near perfect dessert. A delightful story about a young woman, who saves a man from a subway train, is mistaken for the man's financee while he's in a coma, and then falls in love with his brother! It's not profound, but it's a wonderful movie. (9)

The Wings of the Dove—A delightful unveiling of the intrigues flowing from the romance between a beautiful young woman and an engaging young man in (1910) London. But they'd also like to have money. A friend who is dying (it is discovered) enters the relationship—a rich friend. Excellent acting, careful direction, and handsome photography enhance the story. (8)

Merle Good has been reviewing films for nearly 30 years. The films listed here are ones he has reviewed since the publication of **Festival Quarterly's Video Guide, 1974-1994.**

Our Sponsors

About the Editors

Merle Good has authored numerous articles, books, and dramas about Mennonite and Amish life. Among his better known writings are Op-Ed essays in *The New York Times* and *Washington Post,* dramas *Today Pop Goes Home* and *Going Places,* children's books *Reuben and the Fire* and *Reuben and the Blizzard,* a novel *Happy as the Grass was Green,* and photographic essays *Who Are the Amish* and *An Amish Portrait.*

Phyllis Pellman Good has also authored many articles and books about Mennonite and Amish life. She served as Editor of *Festival Quarterly* magazine for 22 years. Her books include *Perils of Professionalism, A Mennonite Woman's Life, The Best of Mennonite Fellowship Meals* (her cookbooks have sold more than a million copies), and a children's book *Plain Pig's ABC's: A Day on Plain Pig's Amish Farm.*

The Goods have teamed together on numerous projects through the years. They are executive directors of The People's Place, The Old Country Store, The People's Place Quilt Museum, and Good Books, all based in the Lancaster County village of Intercourse. Among the books they have authored together are *303 Great Ideas for Families* and *20 Most Asked Questions About the Amish and Mennonites.* The Goods live in Lancaster, Pennsylvania, and are the parents of two college-age daughters.